Jessica James, Michael Leister, Christoph Rieger

Inflation-Linked Bonds and Derivatives

The Moorad Choudhry Global Banking Series

Edited by
Moorad Choudhry

Jessica James, Michael Leister,
Christoph Rieger

Inflation-Linked Bonds and Derivatives

Investing, hedging and valuation principles for practitioners

DE GRUYTER

The views, thoughts and opinions expressed in this book represent those of the authors in their individual private capacities, and should not in any way be attributed to any employing institution, or to the authors as directors, representatives, officers, or employees of any affiliated institution. While every attempt is made to ensure accuracy, the authors or the publisher will not accept any liability for any errors or omissions herein. This book does not constitute investment advice and its contents should not be construed as such. Any opinion expressed does not constitute a recommendation for action to any reader. The contents should not be considered as a recommendation to deal in any financial market or instrument and the authors, the publisher, the editor, any named entity, affiliated body or academic institution will not accept liability for the impact of any actions arising from a reading of any material in this book.

ISBN 978-3-11-078737-5
e-ISBN (PDF) 978-3-11-078742-9
e-ISBN (EPUB) 978-3-11-078747-4
ISSN 2627-8847

Library of Congress Control Number: 2022946063

Bibliographic information published by the Deutsche Nationalbibliothek
The Deutsche Nationalbibliothek lists this publication in the Deutsche Nationalbibliografie; detailed bibliographic data are available on the internet at http://dnb.dnb.de.

Cover image: Nikada/E+/Getty Images
Typesetting: Integra Software Services Pvt. Ltd.
Printing and binding: CPI books GmbH, Leck

www.degruyter.com

Contents

Foreword

In 1992 I joined Hoare Govett Securities, a UK merchant banking institution with a highly regarded "old school" reputation, and after a brief apprenticeship of sorts moved up to the Fixed Income desk run by the legendary Sean Baguley. In due course the firm had set itself up as gilt-edged market makers, and I was delighted to be placed on the short-dated gilts/money markets desk. As such, I didn't have much to do with "Linkers," which were the responsibility of the long bond trader.

I can't deny being relieved, initially, that I didn't have to price them. To me they were strange beasts, even more problematic to value than some of the exotic illiquid high coupon gilts that were within my bailiwick (can one imagine a UK sovereign bond with a 14% or 15% coupon today? I was not sad to see those two old stocks mature, in 1996 and 1997 respectively!). But an "index-linked" security? What was that all about?

In fact, as I was to learn soon enough, index-linked bonds are very much sought-after investment products, particularly by longer-dated investors such as pension fund managers, who have an objective to protect their clients' investments against the ravages of inflation.

As I write these words, "ravage" is no longer an over-emotive word to use, because inflation is very much back on the financial markets agenda. Double-digit inflation levels are prevalent on both sides of the Atlantic, indeed all over the world. Persistent inflation is a pernicious thing, eating away consumers' spending power as well as the value of their savings. An ability to invest in an inflation-protected product, or to hedge against inflation risk, is a very value-added offering in the markets.

And had I possessed this book back in the 1990s, when admittedly the markets looked somewhat different compared to today, far from being apprehensive I would have approached the task of running the Linker book with relish! The authors have produced an exceptionally fine text that de-mystifies every aspect of the index-linked bonds and derivatives markets. Anyone, and everyone, involved in any aspect of this market, be they issuer (borrower), investor, market maker (dealer) or structurer, will benefit from reading this book. It is so accessibly written, so thoughtfully illustrated, so clearly explained, that I am tempted to say it is the last word on the subject!

My favourite chapter is Chapter 3, "Inflation-linked Products and Curves," which provides a thorough description of both cash and derivative index-linked instruments. Reading it reminded me of the longest-dated product that I have ever personally come across: it was when I was at RBS Global & Banking & Markets Division Treasury, and involved a 70-year inflation-linked derivative transacted with a local authority counterparty. Seventy years! That takes some risk management 😉 !

https://doi.org/10.1515/9783110787429-203

I read this book with a smile on my face, such a great job have the authors done in explaining this exotic, but very relevant and important, asset class. A truly high class work, written by genuine professionals at the top of their game. I commend it to you.

Professor Moorad Choudhry
Surrey, England
December 2022

Introduction

We live in a changing world where inflation is staging a frightening comeback! Since 2008, inflation throughout most of the developed world has hovered close to zero, raising the specter of disinflation and its associated problems. Nothing, not massive monetary and fiscal stimulus, exchange rate gyrations or political upheavals seemed to be able to change it, and it came to gradually deserve the title of the "new normal."

But was this really so unusual, and should we really have expected it to persist? The finest database of inflation in the past comes from the Bank of England, and contains 800 years of the best approximations to inflation year by year, created by scholars of history and econometricians, that can be made from the surprisingly rich records we have available. In the final chapter of the book we graph this data, and it can be seen that long fallow periods of low or even negative inflation were often seen, along with multiple spikes and higher phases, which means that this recent long trough should not raise any eyebrows. While we can certainly make the case that our current world, with its automation and connectivity, differs greatly from the past, a similar argument could probably have been made in every one of the eight centuries in the database. In short, to anticipate that we had reached a new paradigm, a forever period of lowflation and government support, was to make the same mistake that humankind has always made – to assume that things will never change.

Now, Covid and war in Europe have changed everything. Ever since the demise of Lehman Brothers in 2008, the outlook for inflation had almost exclusively been focused on the downside risks for prices and how to deal with the prospect of structural disinflation. These discussions now seem lightyears away. The disruptions on supply chains and consumption patterns triggered by the pandemic together with stimulus packages that came close to helicopter money have catapulted inflation rates to levels last seen in the 1970s.

The subsequent policy tightening of central banks eager to protect their inflation credibility has also reversed the trend of ever lower real yields which in turn has triggered sharp re-pricings across all asset classes.

For inflation markets, it's hard to understate this sudden and enormous change in fortunes. Trading volumes in inflation-linked products have exploded given the seismic change in the demand for these products. At the same time, understanding the information contained in index-linked products on the future evolution of consumer prices has become crucial for investors across all asset classes as central banks tailor their policy responses with a view to anchoring inflation expectations. This exercise is not always straightforward, however, as the specific characteristics of inflation-linked products as well as those of the underlying consumer price indices require specific analytical techniques which go beyond those of the standard of (nominal) rates products.

https://doi.org/10.1515/9783110787429-204

In this book, we condense more than 15 years of dedicated coverage of inflation markets. We hope to provide investors, issuers and policy makers with all relevant tools to navigate inflation markets, starting with the nuts and bolts of consumer price indices to advanced topics like seasonality adjustments and the use of inflation options.

In Chapter 1, "Inflation Indices," we introduce the concept of inflation-linked products and inflation indices, which determine the payouts of these products. We describe the main European inflation index family, the HICP and associated indices, and describe the history of this index which has undergone several revisions over the last decade. We see how well the index represents actual experienced inflation. We then move on to the main US inflation indices, the US CPI and PCE, and discuss how they are constructed and how well they represent US inflation.

In Chapter 2, "The CPI linkage, the Concept of Break-even Inflation, and the Deflation Floor," we build on the on the indices introduced in Chapter 1 and go into the details of how to calculate these reference indices and how index-linked bonds ensure investors receive a certain real return. We then go on to discuss break-even inflation, which links traded inflation products to the real world, and following on from this, the deflation floor, which comprises the unique behavior of products whose strike levels lie close to or at the zero value of actual inflation – the border between inflationary and deflationary environments.

Chapter 3, "Inflation-linked Products and Curves," begins with a discussion of the motivations of market participants for buying inflation-linked products, and how well these products tend to deliver. We go on to look at inflation-linked product supply/demand, volumes and the type of investors who trade them. Linker issuance tends to have a strongly seasonal pattern which we examine. Next we look at inflation curves and introduce the concept of break-even inflation, that level of future inflation at which market participants become indifferent to inflation linked or nominal bonds – in other words, a way to derive what market participants will pay to lock in a value of future inflation. These calculations form the basis of the inflation curve, analogous to a yield curve for underlying interest rates. These give rise to curve-based and spread-based inflation products like asset swaps and other derivatives of the inflation linked market. We outline the mechanics for constructing these inflation curves which are made more complex by the strong seasonality factors.

Chapter 4, "Forwards, Carry and Trading Strategies," begins to go into the reality of trading in this market. Carry is an essential part of trading any curve-based product, and inflation is no exception. It refers to the fact that if a curve stays roughly constant, profits may be made by buying and selling at different curve tenors, and rolling those positions to retain their approximate tenor properties. Even if a curve does not stay constant, this carry element will contribute to profits and losses. We show how carry is calculated for inflation products, which is non-trivial as interest rate carry will also impact valuations. We discuss how carry may be incorporated into trading strategies involving spot and forward trades on the inflation curve. As might be expected, it is essential to incorporate seasonality effects into these calculations and we show how to take this into account.

Moving on to Chapter 5, "Inflation Expectations, Seasonality and Base Effects," we tackle the central issue of future inflation. Where do people think that inflation will go? Up, down, static? While we can extract forward inflation prices from the inflation products, does this actually reflect genuine inflation expectations? And how do we account for the seasonal effects embedded in consumer price indices, like post-Christmas sales or July reductions in the retail sector? Relying on one measure only can be misleading given the various structural and mechanical pitfalls of inflation products. In this chapter, we present a broader set of metrics and cross-checks in order to obtain a robust and comprehensive picture of market-based inflation expectations.

In Chapter 6, "Risk Measures and Risk Premia," we examine the nature of risk in the inflation market. It's usual to assign the work 'risk' to volatility – i.e., price variability, usually related in the literature as the standard deviation of returns. However, the "risk premium" is a subtly different concept, and a consequence of uncertainty. Inflation-linked products trade at a spread to similar nominal counterparts, and this spread is due to both the expected value of genuine inflation, and a risk premium which compensates for the uncertainty surrounding future inflation. Though it is an intuitive concept, it is surprisingly difficult to estimate these two components. In this chapter we go into detail about the nature of both risk measures and risk premia, and illustrate how it is possible to derive values for both under certain assumptions.

Finally in Chapter 7, "Inflation Options," we discuss inflation derivatives and whether their implicit "view" of the future is a useful forecast. Though inflation options have been mentioned before, this chapter treats them in detail. They offer the possibility of extracting an underlying "expected distribution" of future inflation, which is an alluring prospect, especially to investors and policymakers trying to derive probabilities of large inflation moves in the future. However, a deep dive into the nature of this calculation reveals that much of the data should not be relied upon for this purpose; while extracting market expectations about the deflation floor is likely to be well-founded, much of the rest of these derived distributions need to be treated with caution.

We would like to thank Christoph Balz, Bernd Weidensteiner, Rainer Guntermann and Christoph Weil for their significant and important contributions to this book.

Chapter 1
Inflation Indices

Introduction

Inflation-indexed products ("linkers") promise investors a certain real return, including the effect of inflation. The cash-flows of these products are linked to a price index (usually a consumer price index [CPI]), which captures the changes in the prices of goods and services of the country where the product is based. CPIs form the backbone of inflation markets and in this chapter we present the key characteristics and components of the major euro area and US price indices and discuss measurement issues as well as metrics for assessing underlying inflation. The inflation markets are constantly changing and thus metrics for size, flow and product popularity change with time. We have supplied dates for figures where relevant; otherwise the numbers are those extant at the end of 2021/spring 2022.

Euro Area – HICPx

Since its inception in 1998 the European linker market has evolved into a mature and liquid market. In the euro area, the benchmark index is the non-seasonally adjusted HICP ex tobacco (Harmonised Index of Consumer Prices [HICPx]). Tobacco prices tend to distort the index and thus the version of the index that omits them is more widely used.

German, French, Spanish and Italian inflation-linked bonds (ILBs) amount to €620.7bn or about 9.8 percent of government bonds outstanding for these issuers. Not all linkers are alike; France, for example, has linkers outstanding tied to its domestic inflation index (i.e., though they trade in euros they reference the French inflation index not the HICPx) and Italy has about €77.5bn in BTP Italia, which are linked to domestic inflation and target domestic retail investors. See Figure 1.1 for detail.

Inflation swaps referenced to HICPx are actively traded across maturities and inflation options also trade on a regular basis.

HCPIx Versus CPI

As CPIs can vary on a national level, for example due to different calculation methods or coverage of households, HICPx provides a consistent framework across euro area countries.

https://doi.org/10.1515/9783110787429-001

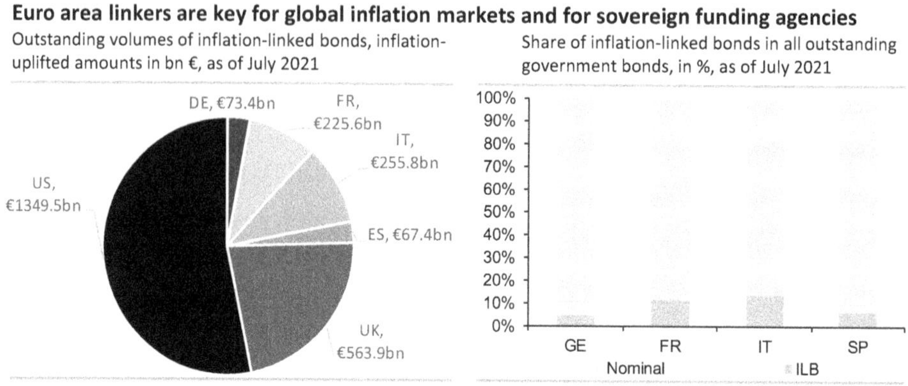

Figure 1.1: Euro Area Linker Volumes.
Source: Bloomberg, Commerzbank Research.

Key differences between HICPx and national CPIs concern the treatment of owner-occupied housing (see also below for details), subsidized healthcare and education costs as well as the geographical coverage of households. The HICP is published on a monthly basis by Eurostat, typically two weeks after the end of the month. It can be found on Bloomberg via the CPTFEMU index. The current reference year for the index is 2015 (index = 100 at this point in time).

The following charts in Figure 1.2 illustrate the major constituents and country weights of HICPx. Note that household final consumption expenditure is the underlying concept for the product as well as country weights that can vary on an annual basis.

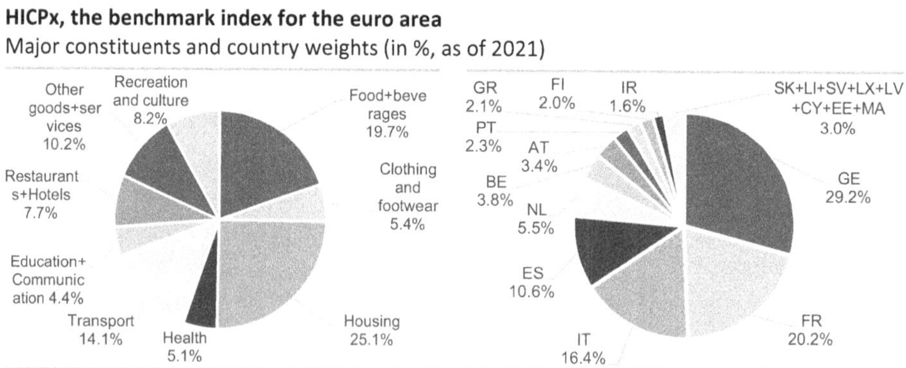

Figure 1.2: HICPx Composition.
Source: Eurostat, Commerzbank Research.

HICPx is obtained by aggregating the respective country indices. There are pronounced differences in the item weights across countries, however, arising from the differences in domestic consumption patterns, as shown in Figure 1.3.

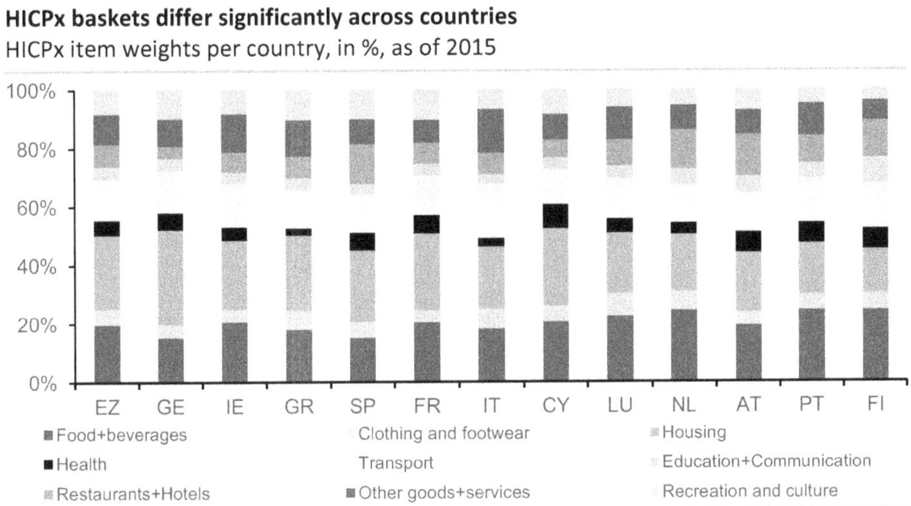

Figure 1.3: HICPx weights per country.
Source: Eurostat, Commerzbank Research.

France – FRCPI

The French CPI (Indice des prix à la consommation [IPC]) is the other major inflation index in the euro area. Outstanding French government bonds linked to FRCPIx amounted to €66.7bn in 2021. The index is published by INSEE (Institut national de la statistique et des études économiques) at about the 22nd of the subsequent month. The current reference year for the index is 2015. It can be found on Bloomberg via the FRCPXTOB index.

The following chart in Figure 1.4 highlights the major constituents:

HICPx Index Events and Their Market Implications

In February 2019, the euro inflation market underwent a set of adjustments following Eurostat's revisions of HICPx series and the first official release of the new series. This had complex knock-on effects that it is worth understanding. The new treatment of packaged holidays (and other items) in the German HICP was at the core of these changes. To mitigate the sharp price swings in this item, they were to be spread throughout the calendar year from then on and no longer recorded in the month they fall due, which was to be achieved via constant rather than variable country weights (say for trips to Greece). These adjustments also resulted in significant adjustments of up to 0.3 percentage points for the euro area HICP.

French CPI: Similar characteristics, but differences to HICPx can be substantial
French CPI ex tobacco item weights, in % as of 2021

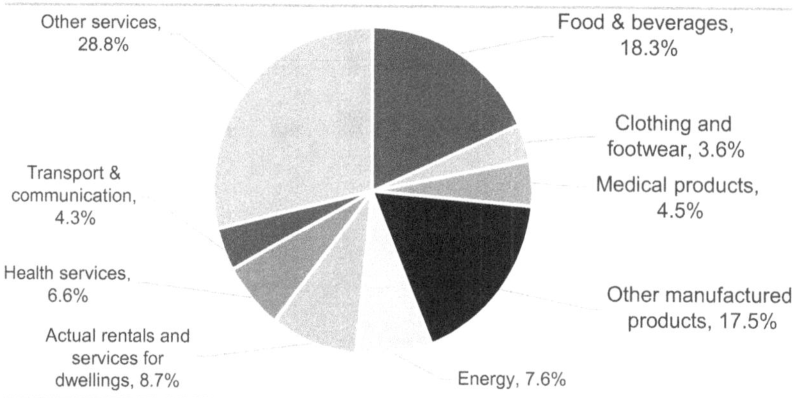

Figure 1.4: French CPI weights.
Source: INSEE, Commerzbank Research.

However, they were only calculated back to January 2015, that is. affecting the base year (2015) and thus required a rescaling of the index to ensure that the average index level for 2015 continued to equal 100. Thus, HICPx levels after 2015 were recalculated and rescaled and those prior to 2015 only rescaled. Eurostat also provided the corresponding "implicit rebasing keys" to force the averages of the revised indices in 2015 back to 100, with 0.99837 being the key for HCIPx.

The Impact and Frictions

Although the year-on-year profile of HICPx was not affected, the seasonal profile changed significantly with the month-on-month changes in November and April particularly affected – and thus also the characteristics of bonds linked to HICPx (inflation-linked bonds or ILBs).

The major sticking point was the rescaling, however. The new HICPx series was significantly above the old (unrevised) series before 2015 by a constant factor and then exhibited sharp month-on-month swings due to the revisions (see Figure 1.5). Thus it was questioned whether Eurostat's "rebasing key" should be applied to pre-2019 values of the unrevised index to ensure that CPI ratios between any two points in time are not affected by the methodological change.

Don't Call It Rebasing!

As euro sovereign debt management offices (DMOs) immediately made clear that base CPIs of their ILBs were not to be revised and future inflation HICPx is lower due to the rescaling, inflation accruals were thus reduced, constituting a windfall for DMOs of some €700mn (i.e., 16.3bp) at the expense of investors.

As derivative cash-flows linked to HICPx were affected in a similar fashion, the International Swaps and Derivatives Association (ISDA) assessed if the changes by Eurostat constituted a rebasing of the index or a material change of the index. If it had been rebased then the whole index would have to be rescaled. ISDA in consultation with market participants concluded that it was a rebasing and recommended that a rebasing key be applied to ensure the "economic integrity of the transactions." One might argue that markets trade the first published index level, that is, that all this is irrelevant. However, rebasings of the first unrevised final published data do matter.

In addition, the documentation of German ILBs contains a very narrow definition of what constitutes a base year revision and the understanding at the time had been that Eurostat would have to officially declare (and calculate) such a rebasing – which seemed unlikely as Eurostat had quickly changed the official wording of its press release and spreadsheet to "back data linking factor," no longer talking of a "implicit rebasing key," presumably to underscore that it is not a base year revision.

Implications

A different treatment by the DMOs and ISDA would have resulted in a split between the cash and derivative market with the one trading on a rescaled series and the other on an unrevised one. Markets were clearly anticipating such a scenario judging by the aggressive moves in early 2019 (sharp swap outperformance versus cash).

In the end, such a split was avoided and the inflation market accepted the deflationary one-off event resulting from the methodological HICPx changes.

Does the HICPx Underestimate Inflation?

How strong is inflation in the euro area? According to official statistics, the HICPx inflation rate in 2020 was 0.3 percent. Excluding the always very volatile prices for energy, food and alcohol, the increase in the so-called core inflation rate was only modestly higher at 0.7 percent. However, it is widely believed that these figures underestimate the increase of the cost of living. Unlike many other countries outside the euro area and also unlike some national price statistics such as those in Germany, the Harmonised Index of Consumer Prices (HICPx) for the euro area does not include the cost of owner-occupied housing.

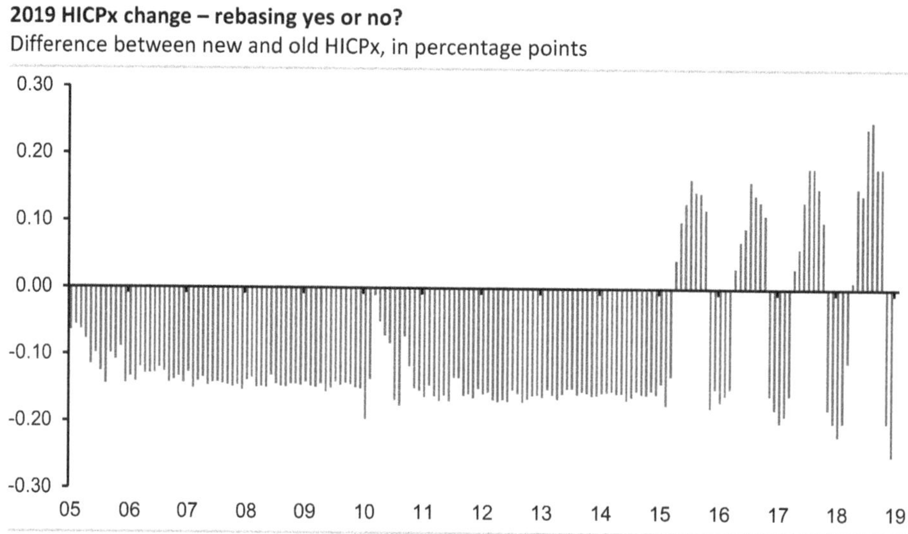

Figure 1.5: HICPx change.
Source: Eurostat, Commerzbank Research.

Proponents of a change of the HICPx to include this factor often refer to the Price Index for Owner Occupied Housing (OOH), calculated by Eurostat, which has grown significantly more than the HICPx since 2015 (Figure 1.6).[1] In the first three-quarters of 2019, these costs were 3.2 percent higher than in the same period of the previous year, while the HICPx grew by only 1.3 percent over the same period, and core energy – which usually takes center stage – by just under 1 percent. If the OOH had been included in the HICP,[2] the core inflation rate would have been 0.4 percentage points higher on average since the beginning of 2016. In the third quarter of 2019 the core rate would have been 1.3 percent, not 0.9 percent.

The boom in real estate markets is responsible for the sharp increase in the OOH in Figure 1.6. In most countries, the weights of the cost of buying or building new housing units – that is, the purchase price and the associated costs – have been from

1 Eurostat publishes figures for the OOH only for individual countries (with the exception of Greece, for which no data on house prices are provided). We used the same country weights used in the aggregation of national HICPs when calculating a euro area aggregate.

2 In determining the weight of the OOH in "broader" HICPx, we were guided by the share of imputed rents for apartments in private consumption in the euro area. This amounted to 13.3 percent in 2018, including maintenance expenses, which are also included in the OOH. In the HICPx without energy, food, alcohol and tobacco, this would result in a weight of about 18 percent.

Costs for owner- occupied housing increasing more than other prices
Quarterly figures, change on year in %; core inflation rate: HICPx w/o energy, food, alcohol and tobacco, OOH: Owner Occupied Housing price index

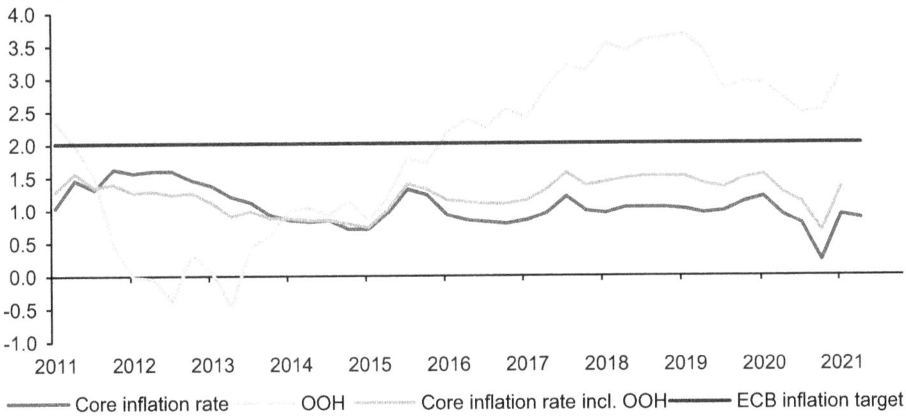

Figure 1.6: Owner Occupied Housing (OOH) vs other indices.
Source: Eurostat, Commerzbank Research.

70 percent to 90 percent, making up the lion's share of this index (see Figure 1.7).[3] Only in Finland do these costs account for less than half of the index, while the weight of other costs such as repairs and insurance are about 53 percent.

Late Availability of House Prices

This high weight of house prices in the OOH and their late availability are strong arguments against integrating the OOH into the HICPx. It's true that data for house prices are available today earlier than a few years ago, but still much later than the prices of the goods and services currently included in the HICPx. While preliminary HICP figures are available with little delay, house prices, and thus the OOH, are only available after a quarter or more. Thus, if the OOH were included, inflation figures could only be published with a considerable delay, or the figures could be significantly revised after a few months, which is unlikely to be desirable.

In addition, it's questionable whether the integration of the OOH into the HICPx would really result in a better measurement of the "actual" price development. After all, when buying a property, you do not only buy a place to live, but you also invest

3 The OOH only takes into account newly built houses or those bought by a private household from an enterprise or from the state. Thus transactions between households are not covered, which means that the purchase of existing houses in most countries has a negligible weight in the OOH.

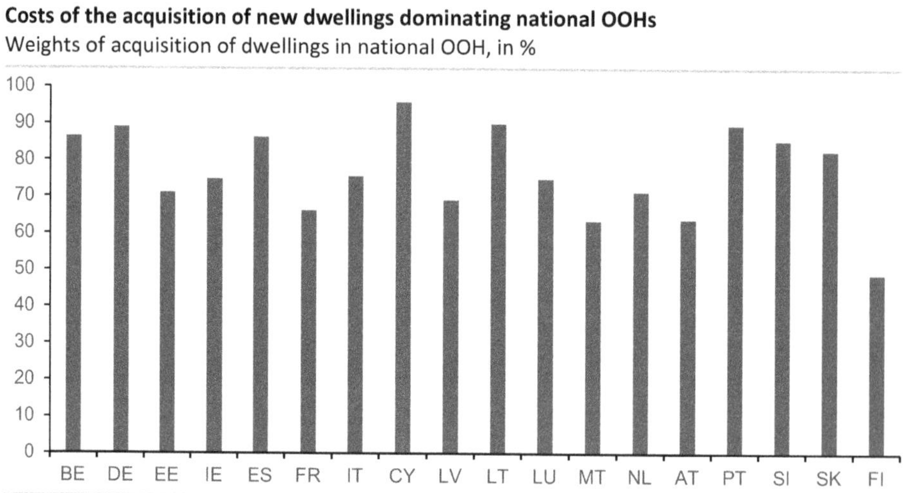

Figure 1.7: New Dwellings Acquisition Weights.
Source: Eurostat, Commerzbank Research.

in an asset. Therefore, a higher purchase price is not necessarily to be equated with higher housing costs, since the sale price expected later may also increase.

Therefore, to measure the cost of owner-occupied housing, the transaction should be divided into two components: investing in an asset and acquiring the right of residence. Only the second part should be included in the HICPx.

Higher Weight for Rents?

The cost of this right of residence can be estimated most easily – and probably most accurately in terms of impact – by looking at the rent for a comparable property. After all, the owner does not receive rent by living in their own property (which they could earn by renting it out), which means that the rent can be said to correspond to the costs.

In practice, these fictitious rents for owner-occupied housing units are estimated differently. In Germany, for example, it is assumed that they develop in line with the rents of real estate actually rented, so that in the end the rents actually paid are included in the index simply with a higher weight.[4] In the United States, on the other hand, a survey shows how these fictitious rents have changed from the

4 For example, rents in the German HICP, which only take into account the rents actually paid, account for only 10.7 percent of the index, while in the national index, which also takes account of owner-occupied residential property, the weight is almost twice as high at 20.7 percent.

point of view of those affected – that is, the residents of owner-occupied residential property. In the US these fictitious rents are mostly in line with the rents actually paid, so the two methods are likely to produce similar results.

If rents had just been given a higher weight in the euro area HICP during recent years, this would hardly have changed the core inflation rate (see Figure 1.8). In December 2019 for example, the core rate would have been just 0.03 percentage points higher, which, in the light of the other uncertainties in the recording of the "right" price trend, for example, the questions relating to a quality adjustment of price developments, is hardly to be regarded as a significant change.

Higher weight for rents increases core rate only slightly
Core HICP (excluding energy, food, alcohol and tobacco), rents, and core HICP with rents weight increased to 20.5 percent from 6.5 percent to reflect OOH, yoy in %

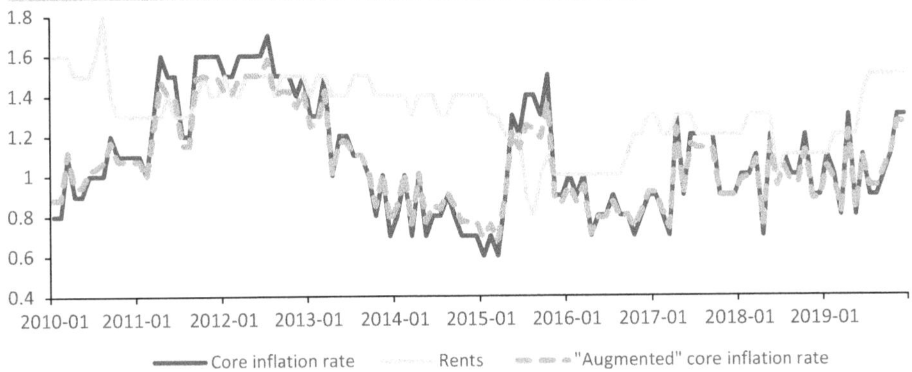

Figure 1.8: Core inflation with augmented rents component.
Source: Eurostat, Commerzbank Research.

ECB Calls for Higher Weight of Rents

In 2021, the ECB advocated for the inclusion of rents following the conclusion of a strategy review. However, the ECB cannot decide on such a change to the HICP alone. The HICP is calculated by Eurostat, and such a change in the survey method must be approved not only by the European Commission, but also formally by the European Parliament and the European Council. Therefore, the change in the HICP is likely to take some time and, for the reasons described above, the effect on the inflation rate is likely to be very limited over the housing cycle. At this date (2022) it has not yet occurred.

US Inflation Indices – A Case Study

In the US, the US CPI plays a similar role to that of the HICPx in Europe. To understand the various US indices and how they relate to one another, let us look at Figure 1.9 to consider a particular period in time when inflation rose sharply.

In May 2021, the US inflation rate jumped to 5 percent. With the post Covid-19 reopening of public life, a wave of price increases swept through the country, with goods and services that saw their prices fall during the pandemic due to declining demand becoming more expensive. Other goods and services saw price rises when shortages occurred post-pandemic. While these effects were stronger than expected, they were not totally surprising.

Inflation rate jumps to 5 percent
Consumer price index, annual rate of change in %, monthly data

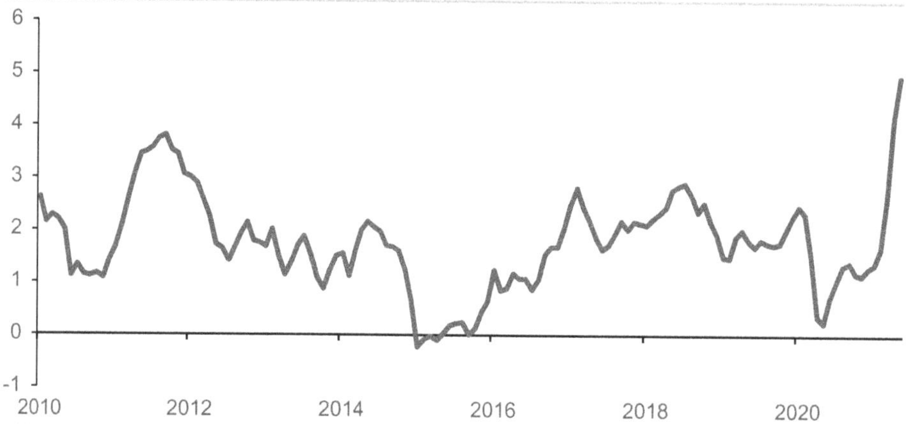

Figure 1.9: Sharp increase in inflation.
Source: BLS, Global Insight, Commerzbank Research.

CPI and PCE Deflator

Probably the two most important US inflation measures are the consumer price index (CPI) and the personal consumption expenditures (PCE) deflator. The latter is less well known to the public, but it is referred to in the Fed's 2 percent inflation target. The Fed prefers the PCE index to the CPI in part because the PCE index is broader.

For example, the CPI measures only the change in prices of expenditures that households themselves pay for, whereas the PCE index targets all goods and services consumed, regardless of who paid for them. This conceptual difference means that some expenditures in the PCE index are outside the CPI. For example, the CPI includes only medical services paid for by consumers out of pocket, while the PCE index includes services paid for by employers and under government health programs such as Medicare and Medicaid. Producer prices (PPI) are used for many of these additional PCE items, while prices according to CPI are also typically used in the PCE index for identical expenditure categories. However, even where the PCE index uses the same prices, differences occur because the two indexes weight the individual expenditure items differently.

Overall, the high weight of rents and imputed rents for owner-occupied homes of one-third is particularly striking in the CPI, while the PCE index takes health care services more into account (see Table 1.1).

Table 1.1: Different indices, different weightings. Weighting of various categories in the CPI and the PCE deflator, in %.

	CPI	PCE
Commodities	**37.3**	**33.4**
Durables	10.9	12.0
Food/Beverages	15.2	7.8
Services	**62.7**	**66.6**
Rent of shelter	33.0	16.9
Medical care services	7.3	16.9
Core	**79.7**	**88.7**

Source: BEA, BLS, Commerzbank Research.

All Draw from the Same Barrel

All inflation indices are essentially based on the same data set, namely the prices collected by the Bureau of Labor Statistics for the consumer price index. This also applies to the so-called core rates, which are used to get a better impression of the underlying price trend. Here, the available data are merely weighted differently or prices that are considered to be of little significance with regard to the inflation trend are omitted altogether. The core indices thus show a section of the general price trend.

Core Inflation: The Workhorse

Classic measures of underlying inflation are the core rates (Figure 1.10), which do not take into account the particularly volatile prices of energy and food. This is because the short-term effects that occur frequently for these goods, such as a poor harvest due to weather conditions or disruptions in oil pipelines, quickly pass through to retail prices without influencing the general price trend. This approach is popular for both the CPI and the PCE index.

Core rate – the workhorse
Consumer price index and deflator of personal consumption expenditures, excluding food/energy, annual rates of change in %. Fed's inflation objective: 2 percent

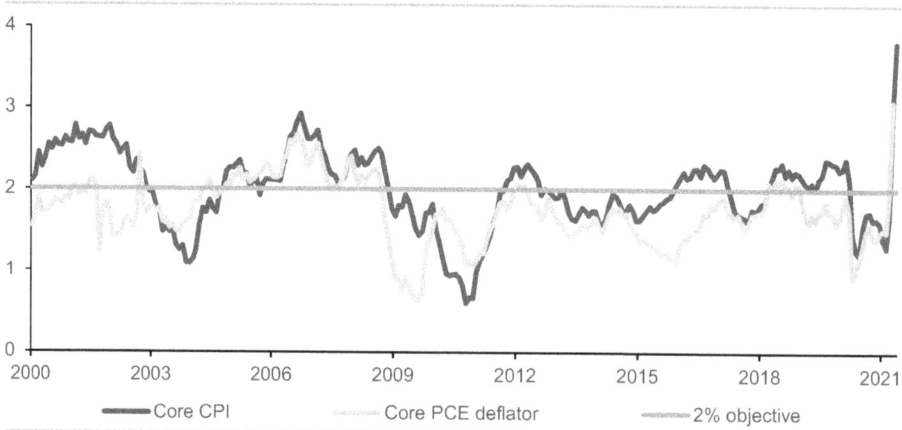

Figure 1.10: Core inflation.
Source: BEA, BLS, Global Insight, Commerzbank Research.

Median CPI

However, excluding the same categories every time when determining the "underlying" inflation is not the only option. Alternatively, one can omit the goods whose prices are fluctuating particularly strongly at that point in time. An analogy to this is the scoring system in figure skating, where the best and worst scores in each case are dropped from the evaluation.

The big question here, of course, is how much you want to trim off the two ends of the price distribution. In the extreme case, one trims the two ends until only the category that lies exactly in the middle of the distribution remains. For 50 percent of the basket (not according to the number of goods, but according to their expenditure-weighted share in the index's basket), prices then rise more sharply than in this category; for the other 50 percent prices rise more slowly. The idea behind this is that the price change of this middle best reflects the true inflation trend. The most prominent example of such a "core index" is the median USA CPI calculated by the Cleveland Fed (see Figure 1.11).

One drawback is that the median often falls into the category of rents and owner-occupied rents because they have a very high weight in the basket of goods. Thus, the median CPI often resembles the rental price trend over longer periods (see Figure 1.11).

Fed's core rates mostly shadow rents
Price indices, monthly rates of change in %

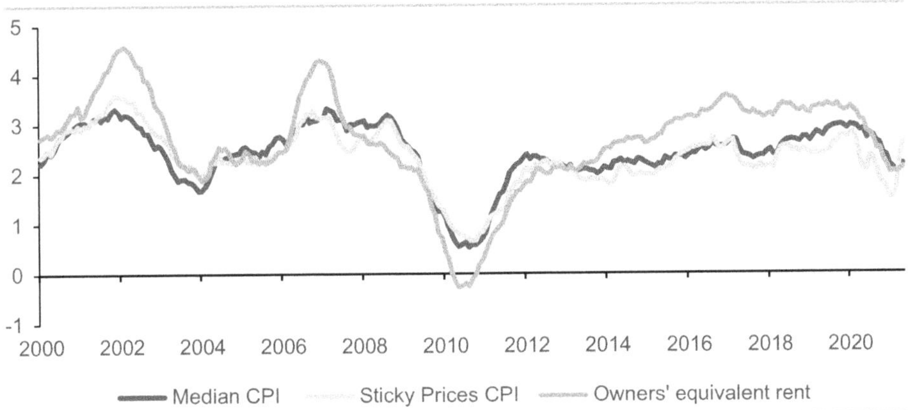

Figure 1.11: Core inflation indices resemble rents.
Source: Fed, Global Insight, Commerzbank Research.

Flexibility and Trimming

Another approach is to classify commodity groups according to the frequency of price adjustment. Some – the most flexible – have frequent price changes, often even daily (gasoline prices, for example). Others, such as rents, are adjusted only at long intervals (from which the name of an index based on these rather inert prices derives – "sticky price index"). Inflation risks increase when sluggish prices follow a steeper upward trend, confirming any increase in more flexible prices. The risk then increases that higher inflation will become entrenched. The Sticky Price CPI calculated by the Atlanta Fed includes about 70 percent of the goods in the overall index. As Figure 1.11 shows, the median CPI and the sticky price index differ little overall though there are periods of divergence.

Alternatively, one omits only those groups of goods that fluctuate particularly strongly. The Dallas Fed applies this procedure to the deflator. Each month, the 24 percent of goods groups with the lowest price increases and the 31 percent with the highest price increases are omitted. The average of the remaining categories weighted by their respective spending shares is then the "Trimmed Mean PCE Deflator." The uneven cut, which appears somewhat arbitrary at first glance, was chosen so that the resulting inflation measure best reflects the underlying trend of the overall index as determined by statistical methods.

The trimmed mean has similar variation to other indices, as we see in Figure 1.12, though it lacks the sharper peaks and troughs. Median CPI and the trimmed scales contain a much smaller share of the goods and services basket than the conventional core inflation indices (the core deflator still represents almost 89 percent of expenditure-weighted items).

Trimmed index shows lower volatility
Core measures of inflation, annual rates of change in %, Fed's 2 percent inflation objective

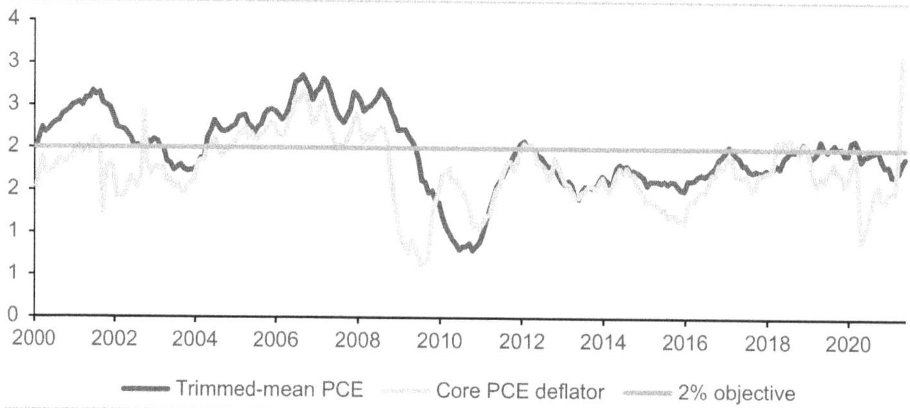

Figure 1.12: Trimmed-mean PCE vs core.
Source: Fed, Global Insight, Commerzbank Research.

What Does All This Tell Us?

In early 2022, the headline indices show the highest inflation rate, followed by the classic core indices, which exclude food and energy prices (see Table 1.2). The rather high rates for the classic core indices are due to the fact that goods particularly affected by

Table 1.2: Inflation rates compared in 2021.
Price indices, annual rate of change in %. Most recent reading, 12 months earlier and average inflation rate for 2010–20.

	Last Reading	Inflation rate	12 months earlier	2010–20
Based on CPI				
CPI	May 21	4.9	0.3	1.8
CPI, core rate	May 21	3.8	1.4	1.8
Median CPI	May 21	2.1	2.7	2.2
Sticky prices CPI	May 21	2.6	2.2	2.0
Based on PCE deflators				
Deflator	Apr 21	3.6	0.5	1.6
Deflator, core rate	Apr 21	3.1	0.9	1.6
Trimmed mean PCE	Apr 21	1.8	1.9	1.7

Source: BLS, BEA, Commerzbank Research.

the Covid-19 crisis and the reopening of the economy are components of these core indices (such as used car prices, which rose sharply).

In contrast, energy and food prices, which are ignored by these core rates, have little to do with the pandemic. Thus, if short-term special effects are to be excluded from the inflation rate, the trimmed measures (trimmed-mean deflator and median CPI) can add value (Table 1.2).

Chapter 2
The CPI Linkage, the Concept of Break-even Inflation and the Deflation Floor

As discussed in the first chapter, all cash-flows of index-linked products are tied to a consumer price index, which captures the changes in the prices of goods and services. In this chapter we go into the detail of how to calculate these reference indices and how index-linked bonds ensure investors receive a certain real return. We then go on to discuss break-even inflation, which links traded inflation products to the real world, and following on from this, the deflation floor, which comprises the unique behavior of products whose strike levels lie close to or at the zero value of actual inflation – the border between inflationary and deflationary environments.

The CPI Linkage

Consumer price indices (CPI or HICPx) are only published with a time lag as the statisticians require time to gather the relevant data and compute the indices. The (unrevised) CPIs (ex tobacco) are therefore applied with a three-month time lag to compute cash-flows in the euro area and most other linker markets.

An example: The Apr-21 HICPx index is used for July 21. To be precise, this index is used for calculating the reference index for the first day of the month, in this example 1 July. Similarly, the May-21 HICPx index will be used as the reference index for August 1. For every trading day in between those dates, a daily reference index is calculated by linear interpolation. This is done via the following formula:

$$RefCPI_{t,m} = CPI_{m-3} + \frac{d-1}{D_m} \times (CPI_{m-2} - CPI_{m-3})$$

where CPI_m denotes the respective lagged price index level, D_m the number of days in the settlement month and d the respective day of the settlement month.

For example, the Apr-21 HICPx (used for July 1) is 106.69, the May-21 index (applied to August 1) 106.97. The reference index for July 12, 2021 is therefore 106.78935 (note that the convention is to calculate the index to the 5th decimal). The reference index for the first settlement day of an index-linked bond is called the base index.

The question of how much inflation has taken place since a bond was launched is measured by the progression of the reference index relative to the bond's base index level. In order to capture the inflation accrual between two points in time, the

https://doi.org/10.1515/9783110787429-002

index ratio (IR) is calculated. This ratio is the key concept linking the real and the nominal world.

$$IR = \frac{CPI_{Settle}}{CPI_{Base}}$$

The Index Ratio and Inflation Compensation

All cash-flows will be adjusted by the index ratio on the respective payment date. For example, the full invoice price of a linker trading at clean price of 110, accrued interest of 5 and an IR of 1.1 is equal to (110+5)*1.1 = 126.5.

This inflation uplift can be highly significant and influence total return considerations, in particular for short-dated or seasoned inflation-linked bonds (ILBs).

Assuming positive inflation throughout the life of the bond (i.e., a positive inflation accrual), coupon payments and the principal thus increase in line with prices over time (see Figure 2.1). In this way, investors get compensated ex-post for the loss of purchasing power. While the future cash-flows and thus the return of an index-linked bond is uncertain in nominal terms as future inflation is unknown, the return is certain in real terms, because it is equal to the coupon of the linker (assuming no default of the issuer). On the other hand, nominal bonds offer a certain return in nominal terms, while real (i.e., inflation-adjusted) returns are uncertain.

Note also that for Euro linkers the inflation-uplift on the principal will never be below one – even in the case of deflation. In other words, the principal amount is floored at par. This does not apply to the coupon, however, as discussed later in this chapter.

Inflation-linked bonds: Ex-post inflation compensation ensures a certain real return ex-ante
Coupon and principal payment on a 10y bond with real and nominal coupon of 1.5 percent, assuming 2 percent inflation until maturity

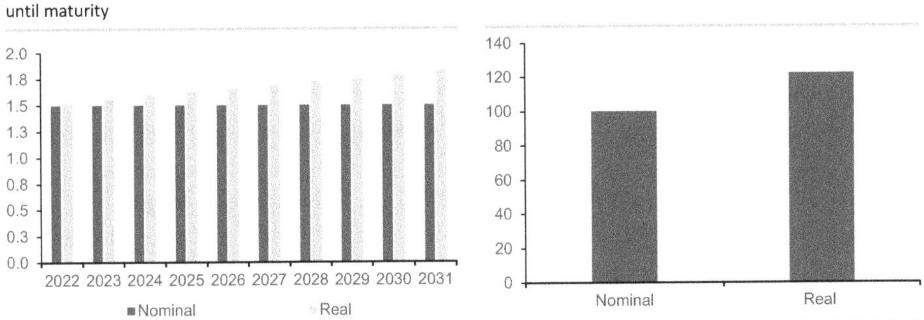

Figure 2.1: Inflation linked bonds real and nominal returns.
Source: Commerzbank Research.

Real Versus Nominal Returns

Care has to be applied when interpreting real yields of index-linked bonds. Just as for nominal bonds, real yields are typically derived from clean. Hence, they do not reflect the inflation accrual and can therefore provide a misleading yield to maturity – or internal rate of return (IRR) – in nominal terms.

This is particularly relevant when comparing the yield/IRR of a nominal and an index-linked bond, as ignoring the inflation accrual can provide a false picture of the relative (expected) total returns of the bonds in nominal space. This applies particularly for seasoned ILBs with (very) short residual maturity: as the clean price gets mechanically pulled to par, the inflation compensation on the principal (which will be paid out at maturity) is gaining considerable value and hence has to be included in yield/relative value assessments, particularly versus nominal bonds, which just get pulled to par.

To obtain the nominal yield/IRR (r_N), the NPV of the inflation-uplifted cash-flows of the ILB have to equal its all-in (inflation-uplifted) dirty price, similarly to the yield of a nominal bond. Technically this is achieved via the following formula:

$$P_{All-in} = \sum_{t=1}^{T} \frac{CPN \times IR_t}{(1+r_N)^t} + \frac{100 \times \max\{IR_t, 1\}}{(1+r_N)^t}$$

Note that to compute the above formula, CPI forecasts for the cash-flow dates are required. While this can become a rather tedious exercise (primarily due to seasonality as we discussed in Chapter 3), market practice is to focus on the real yield to maturity of a linker r_{RY}. The latter does not require CPI forecasts and is computed as follows (as for nominal bonds):

$$P_{All-in} = \sum_{t=1}^{T} \frac{CPN \times IR_t}{(1+r_{RY})^t} + \frac{100}{(1+r_{RY})^t}$$

This is also known as the Canadian model and market prices and yields are typically quoted this way (though without accrued interest, similar to nominal bonds). When buying an ILB, the investor nonetheless has to pay the inflation-uplifted price.

It is possible to calculate the all-in price of a linker on Bloomberg, which in turn can be translated into a robust yield-to-maturity for break-even analysis via the Bloomberg function YAS <GO>.

The Concept of Break-even Inflation

Break-even inflation represents the link between the nominal and the real world.

The Fisher Equation

While linkers shield investors ex-post from inflation, nominal bonds also provide a certain degree of ex-ante protection against inflation. Below we give a slightly simplified version of the famous Fisher equation, which highlights the fundamental link between real and nominal yields:

$$\text{nominal yield} = \underbrace{\text{real yield} + \text{inflation expectation} + (\text{liquidity premium} + \text{risk premium})}_{\text{break-even inflation}}$$

This concept helps us to get a handle on the following question: how much inflation is needed for investors to be indifferent between holding index-linked and nominal bonds, that is, to break-even?

Interpreting Break-evens

Break-evens can be interpreted in a number of ways (without accounting for the deflation floor and various risk premia, which we will cover later in this chapter and cover in Chapter 6, respectively).

- **Market-implied inflation expectations:** Break-evens indicate how much inflation the market expects over a given period of time (i.e., the expected annual average rate). For example, a rise in break-evens indicates that the market is adjusting its inflation expectation to the upside. As inflation-linked products are traded across the full range of maturities, forward inflation expectations can be readily calculated (e.g., 5y5y, which captures the average annual inflation over five years starting in five years).
- **Inflation benchmark:** Break-evens are a valuable yardstick to put inflation views into context. If an investor views the markets' inflation expectations as too low, linkers are more attractive than their nominal peers
- **Tradable product:** Interpreting break-evens as simply a spread between two bonds allows for direct trading of the markets' implied inflation expectation.

Break-even Inflation in Practice

In theory, break-even inflation requires that all coupons of the linker would have to be uplifted by the projected CPI level – that is, the expected nominal cash-flows would have to be calculated and discounted with a corresponding nominal rate.

In market practice, break-even inflation is simply calculated as the spread between the nominal and real yield of instruments with similar maturity and credit quality.

Which nominal bond should be used to compute the break-even rate? There is no mechanical rule to determine the nominal counterpart of an ILB, although it should typically be from the same issuer or of similar credit quality and match the ILB's maturity as close as possible. As new ILBs are typically issued at lower frequency than nominals, switching to the on-the-run nominal comparator is often advisable for calculating the spot break-even level, particularly if curves are steep and in longer maturities.

The left-hand chart in Figure 2.2 shows the break-even rate between the DBRei 0.5% Apr30 and a linear interpolation of two nominal bonds on the German curve, that is, the on-the-run DBR Feb30 and DBR Apr31. The interpolation aims to overcome the maturity mismatch of the bonds (in addition to the curve shape, maturity mismatches can significantly impact ILBs and thus break-evens due to seasonality effects, as we will discuss in Chapter 5).

Break-even curves are typically upward-sloping (see the right-hand chart in Figure 2.2), reflecting higher term and inflation risk premia with increasing maturity.

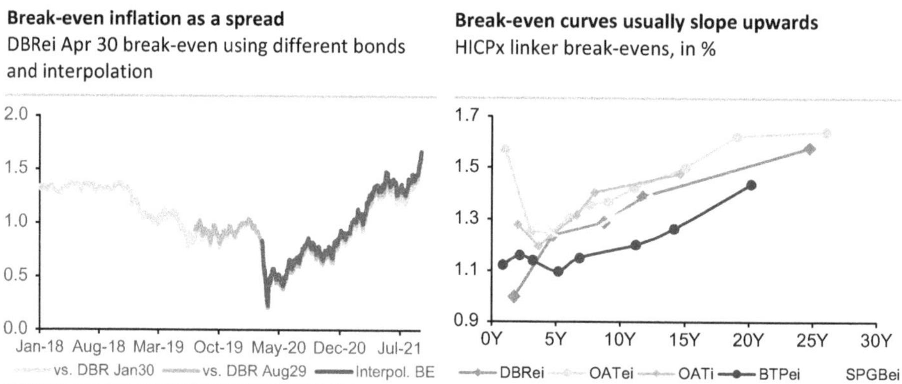

Figure 2.2: Break-even rates and curves.
Source: Commerzbank Research.

The Deflation Floor

Varying figures have brought the design of index-linked products into focus over the past years. Getting a handle on the deflation floor embedded in linkers is also important when pricing new issues and for assessing the relative value of linkers.

The Basics

By construction, all cash-flows of index-linked bonds are adjusted by the index ratio (IR). The IR measures the cumulative inflation accrual since the bond was issued. Technically it equals the reference index for any particular date (e.g., euro area HICPx on April 1, 2021) relative to the reference index at the issue date of the linker, as discussed above.

Assuming positive inflation throughout the life of the bond, coupon payments and the principal therefore increase in line with the (unadjusted) price index. In this way, investors get compensated ex-post for the loss of purchasing power. Likewise, the IR drops in the case of falling prices. Thus, an investor entering a long position in linkers during a disinflationary environment would face a downward adjustment on the cash-flows of the bond and therefore incur negative returns.[1]

Deflation Floor as a Put Option on the CPI

To protect investors from redemption below par, inflation-linked government bonds in the euro area as well as in Sweden and the United States contain a par deflation floor. The floor ensures that investors receive par if the IR is less than one at maturity. In other words, the principal will not fall below 100 percent of the purchase price even in the case of cumulative deflation over the life of the bond.

The deflation floor thus represents a put option on the price index with a strike price equal to the base index of the bond, or alternatively to an IR of one. It is important to note that the coupon is not protected and can go to zero.

An Example

A simple example illustrates the underlying mechanics. Suppose a linker was issued five years ago with an initial maturity of ten years. The current IR of the bond is assumed to be 1.1, implying that average annualized inflation since issuance was close to 2 percent. Now, if the IR is 0.97 at maturity, the floor applies, and the investor will receive par. In the case of an IR equal to 1.05, falling consumer prices between the trade and maturity date would be insufficient for the floor to be in-the-money.

1 Note that investors are often exposed to month-on-month disinflation given the seasonality of underlying price indices (e.g., falling HICPx in January and July). This gives rise to negative carry.

Why is the Deflation Floor Important?

Getting a handle on the deflation floor embedded in euro linkers is important when pricing new issues or assessing the relative value of index-linked bonds. That said, the deflation floor has not received too much attention given the steady rise in inflation indices (i.e., positive inflation rates) observed over the past decades. Likewise, most euro linkers were issued some time ago, in an environment of lower HICPx levels compared to today, as inflation has been positive since their various launch dates.

These seasoned linkers therefore have IRs significantly above 1 (see Figure 2.3). The deflation floor thus tends to be far out-of-the-money and its implicit value is close to 0 for seasoned EMU linkers.

However, the disinflation in major economies 2009–2021, including repeated negative CPI prints, have brought renewed focus to the embedded deflation floor. Likewise, for recently issued linkers the IR is close to 1 and has even temporarily dipped below 1 in some cases, which could imply a substantial value for the deflation floor.

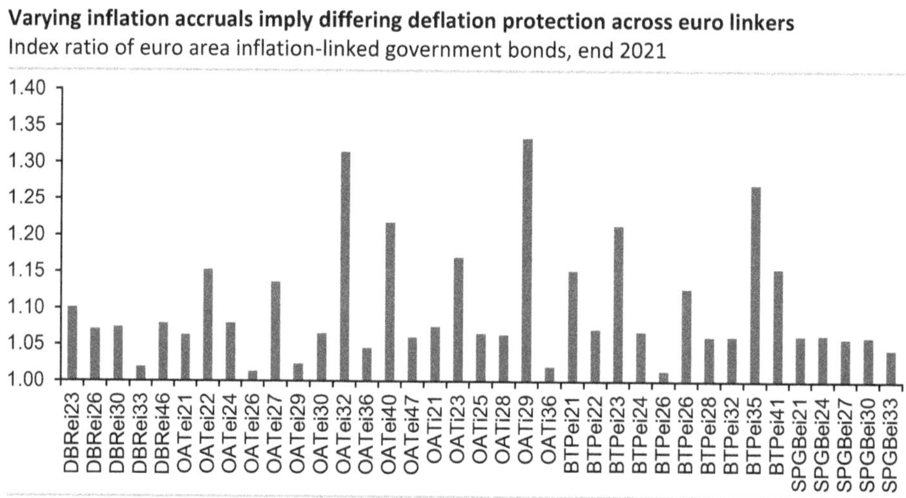

Figure 2.3: Euro area ILB Index Ratios.
Source: Bloomberg, Commerzbank Research.

What Drives the Value of the Deflation Floor?

The inflation accrual since issuance (i.e., the index ratio) determines by how much the deflation floor of a given linker is out-of-the-money. It also makes it possible to quantify the annualized deflation prior to maturity, which would be necessary for the deflation floor to be in-the-money (see Figure 2.4). This enables investors to quickly put the degree of protection into context.

Floor value differs across euro linkers
Annualized CPI decline until maturity necessary for the deflation floor to be in-the-money, in %, end 2021

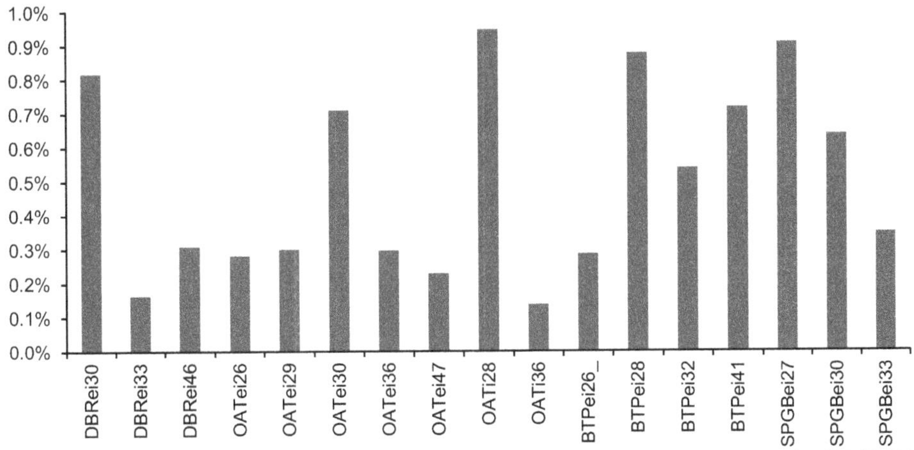

Figure 2.4: Deflation floor.
Source: Bloomberg, Commerzbank Research.

CPI Options to Assess the Floor Value

The value of the deflation floor embedded in inflation-linked bonds can be estimated via the inflation derivatives market where zero-coupon deflation floors are traded in maturities out to ten years (see also Chapter 7 for inflation options and their applications).

These OTC floors pay the difference versus par if the index ratio is below 1 at expiration and 0 otherwise. In the case of the OATei Jul24, for example, the floor was worth *circa* 41cents or 3.8bp at its launch. As the bond holder is implicitly long the floor, this biases the "true" inflation expectation embedded in the break-even rate upward as the ILB's real yield would be higher without the floor (similar to the inflation risk premium covered in Chapter 6). The floor value can therefore substantially impact the relative value of index-linked bonds.

As with any other option, the value of the deflation floor increases with rising volatility. This can be seen by the rising probability of deflation as implied by HICPx options during the stress periods end-2011 and mid-2012 as well as in 2015/2016 and during the pandemic, when the option-implied deflation probability rose above 30 percent (see Figure 2.5). These in turn reflect the cost of insurance against (cumulated) deflation over a five-year horizon. Alongside the fluctuations in inflation expectations, higher volatility and inflation uncertainty have added to this premium increase as investors have become much more sensitive to inflation/deflation (tail) risks since the 2008 financial crisis. More recently (in 2022), higher inflation expectations have added their own twist to the story.

Risk Aversion as Another Key Factor

Risk aversion also significantly impacts the floor value. Deflation typically occurs during macroeconomic shocks. Such shocks are more likely in the case of financial market stress. "High inflation" in contrast typically occurs in a positive economic environment. There is therefore a close interaction of inflation/deflation tail risks with credit and liquidity conditions.

Markets were pricing such a "meltdown scenario" of collapsing prices and output in combination with systemic stress after the Lehman Brothers' collapse in 2008 as well as at the heights of the debt crisis in summer 2012 and the Covid-19 pandemic in March/April 2020. Accordingly, the price for deflation protection collapsed in 2021 as global financial conditions recovered alongside growth expectations and market participants were primarily concerned with risks of inflation overshooting.

The market is also significantly more sensitive to deflationary shocks than it is to rising inflation, and empirical studies for the United States show that inflation tail risks are priced much more modestly than deflation tail risks.

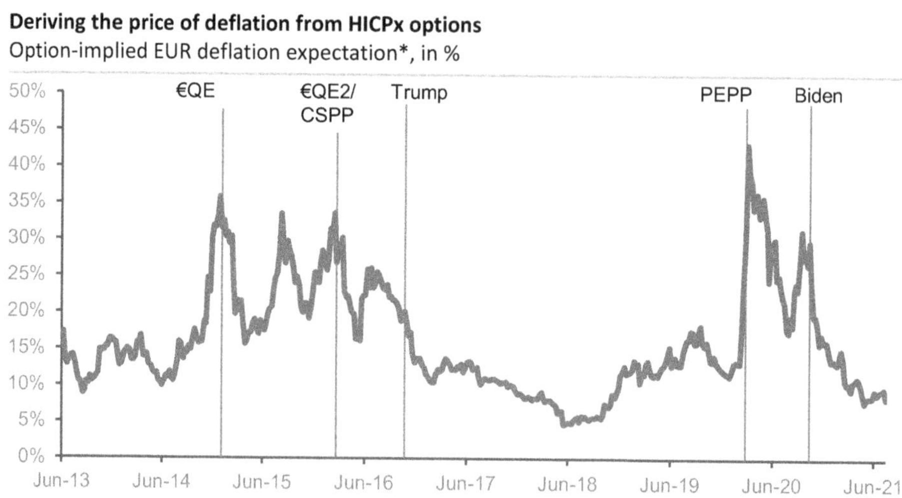

Figure 2.5: Option-derived inflation expectations.
Source: Bloomberg, Commerzbank Research.

Chapter 3
Inflation-linked Products and Curves

Why Issue Linkers?

Resurging inflation fears on the back of Covid-19 are raising the appeal of linkers as a funding instrument. We discuss the major motives for issuing linkers and whether they apply in practice.

The Case for Issuing Index-linked

- **Cost Savings:** As future inflation is uncertain, nominal yields contain an inflation risk premium.[1] By issuing inflation-linked rather than nominal debt, the issuer saves this risk premium over the life of the bond. Most linkers also have an embedded deflation floor that protects investors against redemption below par. The DMOs thus sell deflation floors when a new linker is issued. The resulting premium and the potential cost savings can be significant, in particular as deflation risks are priced much more aggressively than inflation tail risks on the options market.[2] Another popular argument is that markets tend to overestimate inflation, which allows DMOs to capture these excessive inflation expectations. The protracted lowflation environment over recent years, including a negative inflation risk premium, have weakened these arguments, however. The head of the Spanish DMO Pabloe de Ramón-Laca Clausen, for example, explicitly referred to low levels of break-evens as an argument against issuing new benchmark bonds in early 2021.
- **Asset-liability matching:** Governments are naturally long inflation as taxes on income and consumption are levied in nominal terms. Issuing linkers and thus linking liabilities to inflation allows a better matching of public revenues and expenditures. This reduces the government's financial risks.
- **Reduced deficit volatility:** Inflation is typically positively correlated with the budget balance, as inflation tends to be higher during episodes of strong economic growth, which in turn imply higher revenues and lower expenditures. Therefore, lower interest costs on index-linked debt can serve as a stabilizer during disinflationary contractions.

1 Nominal yield – real yield = Inflation expectation + Inflation risk premium + liquidity premium + other premia.

2 See, for example, "Deflation risk" from Fleckenstein, Longstaff and Lustig (2013). One explanation is that "high inflation" typically occurs in a positive economic environment, while deflation coincides with macro shocks.

https://doi.org/10.1515/9783110787429-003

- **Broader investor base:** Linker issuance can give DMOs access to new investor classes, which would not invest in the issuer's nominal bonds given their liability structure. Pension funds are a prominent example. Diversifying the investor base and broadening the funding toolbox also reduces pressure on other funding instruments of the issuer.
- **Public benefits:** While reducing costs is a key objective, financing agencies follow a public mandate. Non-tangible social benefits can therefore provide a strong motive for issuing linkers. The latter effectively creates a new asset class, providing investors with an inflation benchmark and hedging instrument of high credit quality.[3] Linkers also enable policy makers to derive a market-based measure for inflation expectations, thereby reducing the risk of policy errors stemming from distorted inflation expectations. Obtaining objective inflation expectations also mitigates distributional effects between borrowers and savers arising from unanticipated inflation.

From Theory to Practice

The extent to which issuers are able to capture these benefits in practice is not straightforward, with cost savings in particular being debatable. Recall that the mandate of public treasuries is to optimize the nominal costs of financing the government's borrowing needs.

The discussion remains open. Various studies argue that linkers are less attractive from that point of view. The Deutsche Finanzagentur (German finance agency) in contrast estimates a cost saving of €2.4bn compared to synthetic nominal funding for the four Bund linkers, which it has redeemed since 2006 (see Figure 3.1).

Linkers are typically less liquid than their nominal counterparts and real yields therefore contain an (il)liquidity premium. While this premium has lost significance with debt crisis receding and the overall decline in liquidity and risk premia on financial markets, stress periods and rising (il)liquidity premia could offset cost reductions and also imply execution risks for new benchmark transactions in such an environment.

Linker Supply and Demand

It is useful to understand the volumes and supply/demand factors underlying inflation-linked issuance in the euro area and to consider the investor structure into index-linked bonds.

3 In economic terms, the government provides a public good by issuing inflation-linked debt.

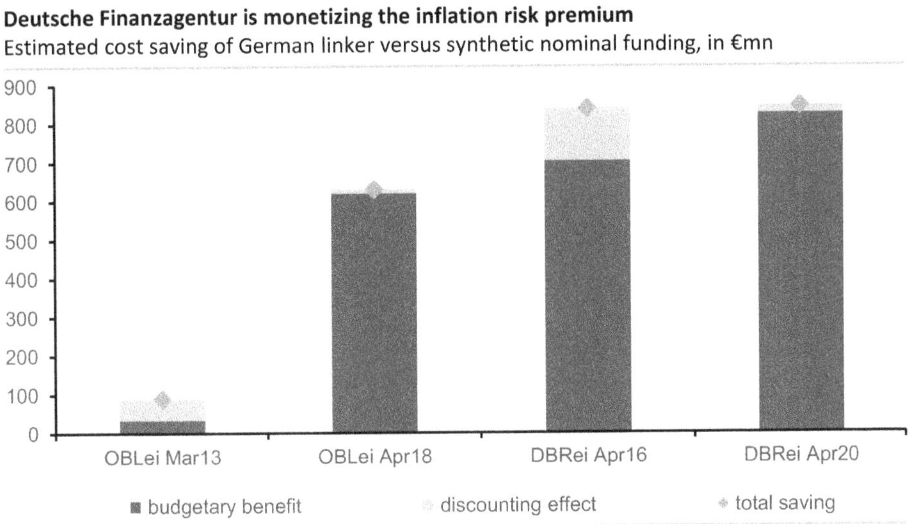

Figure 3.1: Cost saving of Inflation Risk Premium.
Source: Finanzagentur, Commerzbank Research.

Linker Supply

Funding Volumes and Linker Contribution

Annual euro linker issuance has oscillated at about €50bn per year since Spain started its linker program in 2014, as shown in Figure 3.2. France has consistently been the largest issuer with annual supply averaging €20bn, the majority of which is in HICP-linked bonds (weighted-average of 70 percent since 2014).

The contribution of linkers to overall sovereign funding remains comparatively stable with France once more posting the largest contribution. For Spain, the gradual decline primarily owes to the reduced new issue activities, which typically drive year-on-year changes in volumes across all countries, as we see in Figure 3.3.

Funding Composition

Annual linker supply in the euro area shows pronounced seasonal patterns. Figure 3.4 highlights that cumulative supply follows a rather predictable path during the year both in terms of gross as well as in risk-equivalent terms.

Accordingly, the bulk of linker supply is typically placed during the first two quarters when also most of the overall new issue activity is being conducted (Figure 3.5, left chart).

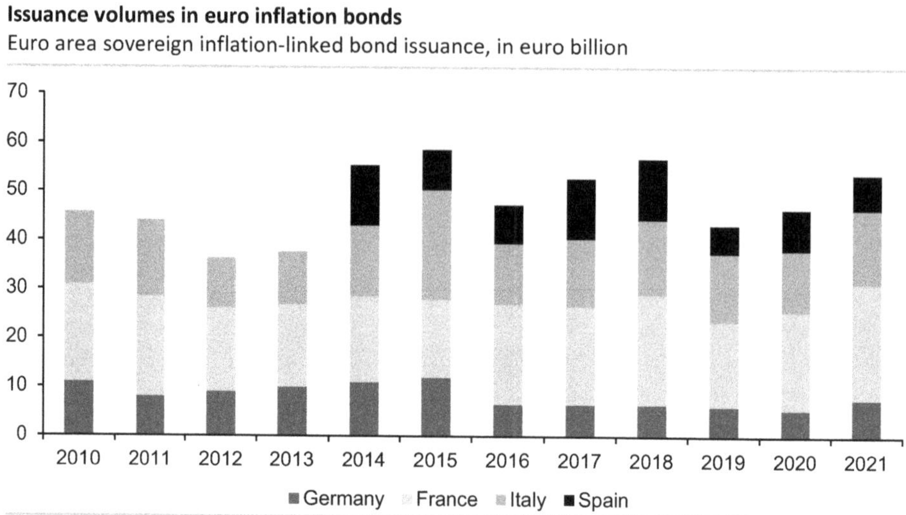

Figure 3.2: Volumes of Euro area ILBs.
Source: DMOs, Bloomberg, Commerzbank Research.

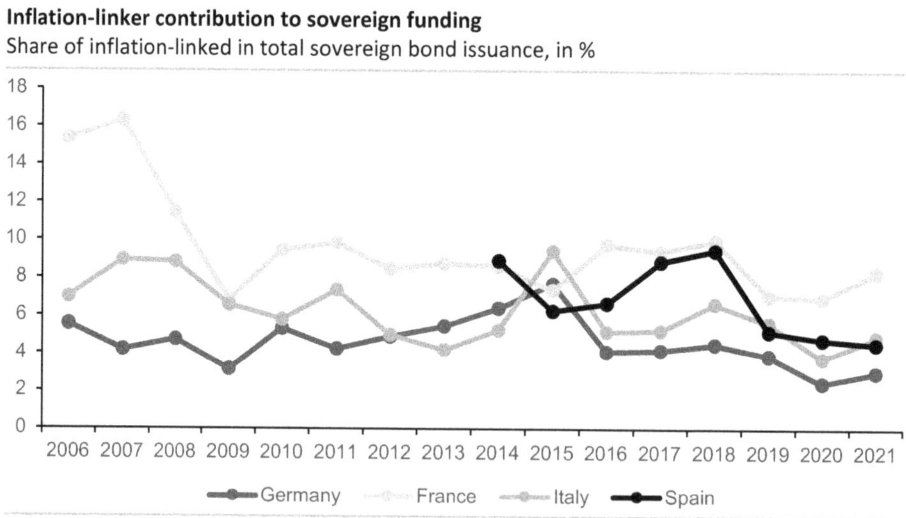

Figure 3.3: ILB share of total sovereign issuance.
Source: DMOs, Bloomberg, Commerzbank Research.

The maturity distribution of euro area linker supply is also stable with the 10y sector absorbing the bulk of the volumes followed by the 5y and 15y sectors (see Figure 3.5, right chart).

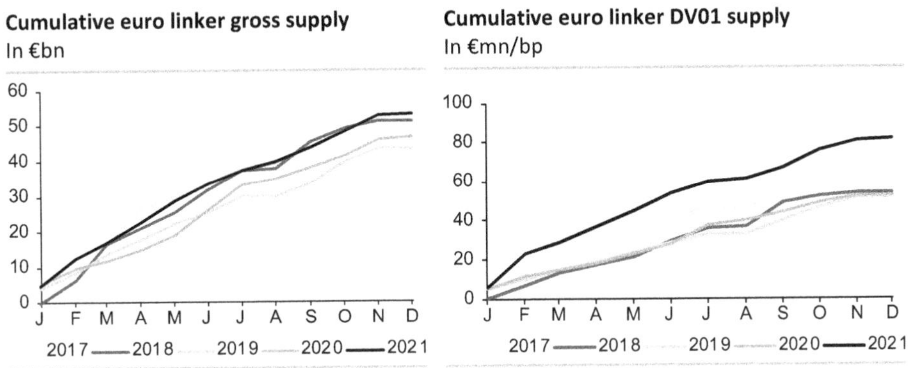

Figure 3.4: Euro ILB supply.
Source: DMOs, Bloomberg, Commerzbank Research.

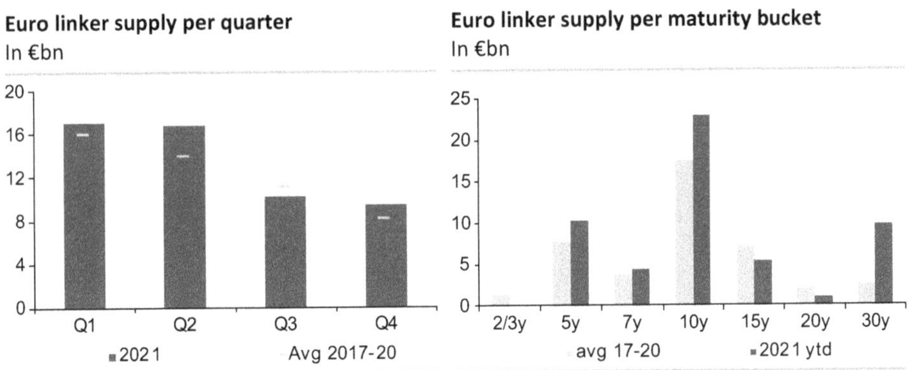

Figure 3.5: Euro ILB supply breakdown.
Source: DMOs, Bloomberg, Commerzbank Research.

The individual countries mirror the aggregate seasonal patterns and maturity trends. Figures 3.6 and 3.7 show the respective issuance progressions through the calendar year. Particularly for Spain and Germany, new benchmark launches contribute substantial amounts and can sometimes distort the comparison to prior years.

Linker Demand

Fund Flows

The return of reflation hopes and overshooting fears on the back of Biden's election have revived the inflation market. This is not only visible in the global break-even rally in 2021, but also in underlying flows.

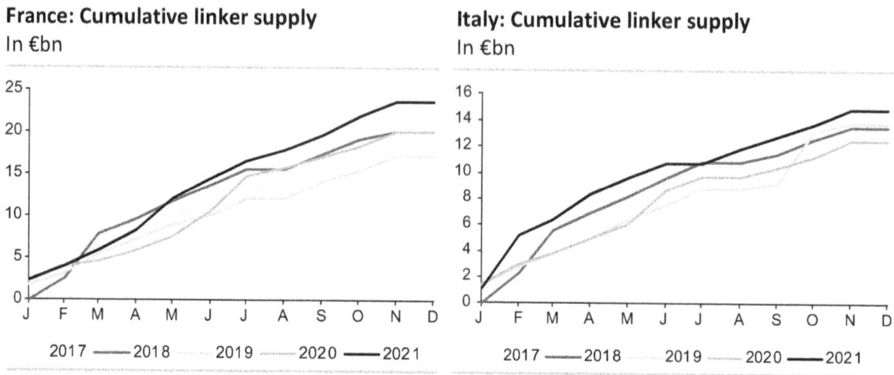

Figure 3.6: France and Italy ILB supply.
Source: DMOs, Bloomberg, Commerzbank Research.

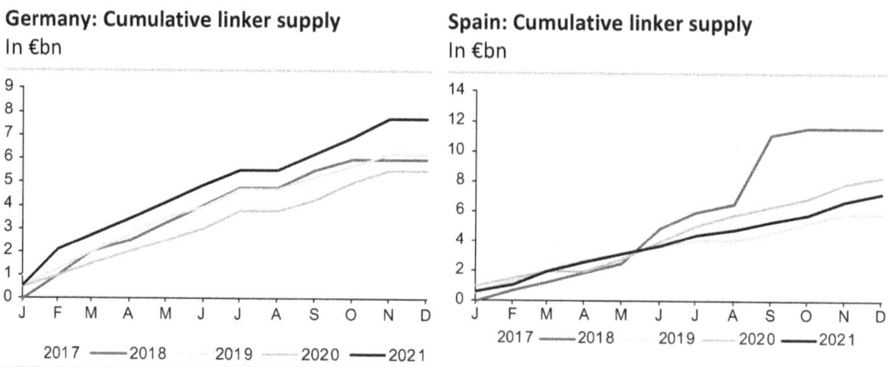

Figure 3.7: Germany and Spain ILB supply.
Source: DMOs, Bloomberg, Commerzbank Research.

Inflows into euro-linker funds have accelerated this year and already are surpassing the totals observable during the previous record years of 2015/2019 (see Figure 3.8).

In addition, the inflows into the euro inflation market since last summer have more than made up for the outflows ahead of the Covid-19 crisis and subsequent deflation fears, both in absolute terms as well as relative to Assets under Management (AuM), as shown in Figure 3.9.

In that regard, the close correlation to fund flows into the US dollar linked market during the initial leg higher underscores the dominance of global factors for the inflation market – in pronounced contrast to the wave of inflows into inflation funds following the euro QE announcements in 2015 and 2016, which was confined to euro products.

Record inflows into the euro linker market after Covid-19
Cumulative flows into euro inflation-linked funds per year, in $bn

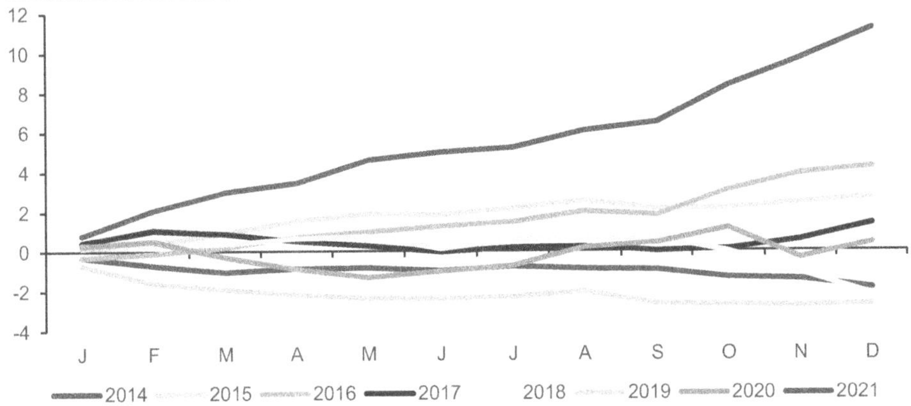

Figure 3.8: Inflows to Euro ILB market.
Source: EPFR, Commerzbank Research.

In addition, these relative inflows are all the more notable in absolute terms as Assets under Management (AuM) of euro inflation funds are 81 percent above levels observable at the peaks in Mar-2017 at currently $33bn.

Are break-even moves backed by investor flows?
Cumulative flows into inflation-linked funds, in % of AuM

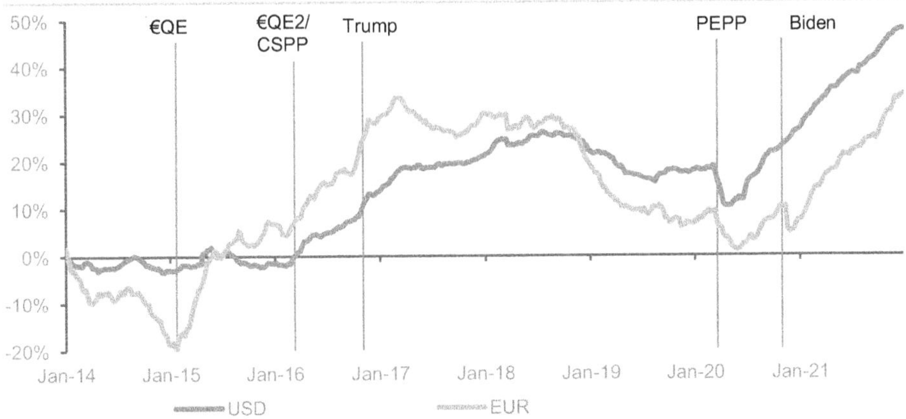

Figure 3.9: Cumulative flows into inflation linked funds.
Source: EPFR, Commerzbank Research.

Linker Syndications

New benchmark linkers are typically launched via syndications, and the distribution statistics allow a granular assessment of the investor base.

For the four most recent benchmark launches, the dominance of domestic investors is the stand- out feature, as shown in Figure 3.10. For one, euro-area-based investors account for more than 50 percent of demand in each transaction, which is probably understated as a significant portion of UK demand is typically on behalf of accounts residing in the euro area. Note also that the Asian investors have hardly been active.

In addition, domestic investors typically constitute the largest investor group, in particular for ultra-long transactions.

Euro syndications driven by domestic investors
Investor split by residence, in % of total

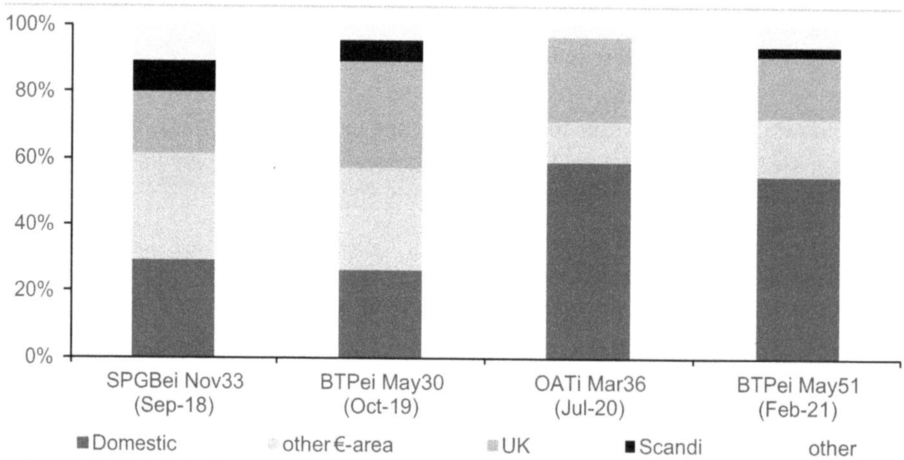

Figure 3.10: Euro syndications split by investor residence.
Source: DMOs, Commerzbank Research.

Inflation Swaps

Inflation derivatives enable investors to isolate and transfer inflation risk. They also provide a straightforward and tailor-made alternative for trading break-evens and assessing relative value. We discuss the key characteristics of inflation swaps and related trading strategies.

A Clean Price for Future Inflation

Inflation linked swaps (ILS) are the favored tool for trading inflation without going into details of the specifics of individual bonds, like seasonality mismatches or supply. Due to the (il)liquidity and credit premia embedded in cash linkers as well as the limited amount of outstanding bonds, break-even rates of inflation-linked bonds are prone to giving biased indications of the inflation expectations discounted by markets.

Inflation swaps mitigate these shortcomings and provide a (comparatively) clean market price for future inflation. They offer good liquidity and are actively traded across a wide range of maturities. According to transaction-based estimates from the ECB the notional amount outstanding of euro area derivatives linked to inflation was €1.3trn as of June 2019, of which 84 percent were linked to HICPx, 15.1 percent to FRCPIx and the 0.9 percent to other euro area indices including the Italian inflation. In addition, almost 45 percent of transactions are done in the 10y and 5y point of the euro ILS curve. Thus, the 5y5y forward seems to deserve its benchmark status for market-based inflation expectations from a liquidity point of view. Note also that ultra-long (10y+) maturities also offer good liquidity given the volume share of *circa* 11 percent (see Figure 3.11).

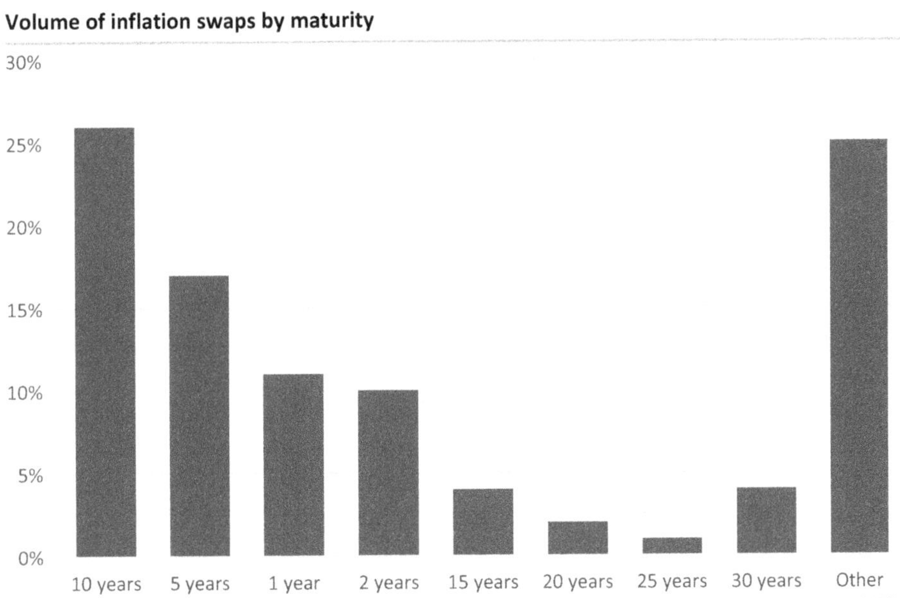

Figure 3.11: Volume of Inflation Swaps by maturity.
Source: Commerzbank Research, ECB.

ILS are therefore a valuable yardstick for putting inflation views into perspective and form the basis for a wide range of investment and business decisions. Inflations swaps are also the building block for the pricing of other inflation-linked instruments and for uncovering trading opportunities as well as the marking-to-market of existing inflation positions.

Inflation Swaps Mirror Break-Even Inflation

Inflation swaps are best compared to break-even inflation. In their plainest form, they are traded as zero coupon swaps. In those, investors swap a fixed rate (in this case the inflation swap rate) for the actual accrued inflation rate occurring over the life of the swap. Due to this design the quoted fixed rate represents the average annual inflation expected over the term of the swap. The final payoff of the swap depends on the reference index value at maturity, as shown in Figure 3.12. Expectations regarding the final index value are thus the key driver of the swap's market value.

A frequent source of confusion arises from the different wording compared to nominal swaps. A receiver position in an ILS implies receiving the accrued inflation rate (i.e., the floating leg) and paying the fixed rate over the term of the swap. An inflation payer will pay the accrued inflation at maturity, receiving the fixed rate.

An example: The 10y zero coupon inflation swap rate on HICPx is at 1.47 percent. An investor paying inflation will receive

$$(1+0.0147)^{10}$$

in ten years' time. In return, he is obliged to pay

$$\frac{HICPx_{t=10}}{HICPx_{t=0}}$$

that is, the actual inflation that occurred since the initiation of the swap. If the actual inflation turns out to be lower on average than the ILS rate agreed at the inception of the swap, the investor will make a profit.

Likewise, if the actual cumulated inflation exceeds the cumulated inflation swap rate agreed upon at the initiation of the trade, the investor will realize a loss if he/she is the inflation payer. This illustrates the similarities with break-even trades: paying the inflation leg in a swap compares to buying a nominal bond and selling an index-linked bond, that is, setting up a break-even tightener in anticipation of lower expected future inflation than currently discounted by the market.

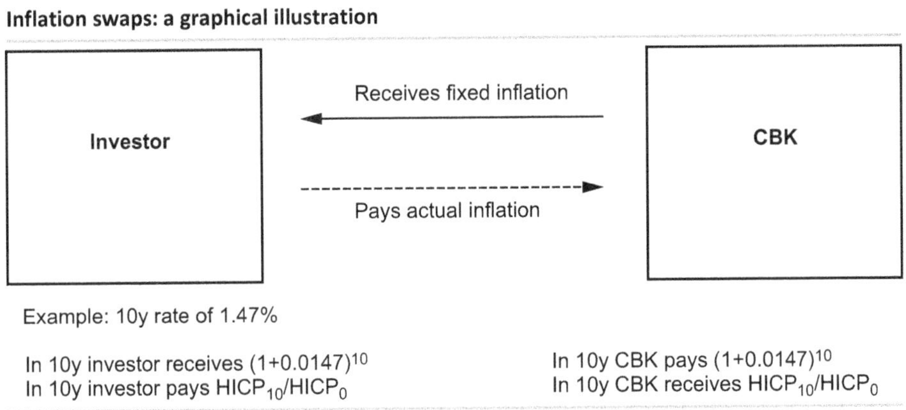

Figure 3.12: Inflation Swap cashflows.
Source: Commerzbank Research.

Base Conventions

As always, it is important to pay close attention to the details, because inflation swaps exist in every conceivable variation. The most common are zero swaps on French, euro area, US and UK inflation. However, swaps with annual payments are also actively traded. Moreover, there are various selected underlying instruments. In addition to establishing and hedging trading positions, inflation swaps are most often used in the creation of tailor-made products, such as inflation-capped Continuous Maturity Swap (CMS) structures.

However, there is a significant difference between swaps based on euro area and French inflation regarding the fixing of the base index for the swap. The HICPx (Harmonised Index of Consumer Prices, ex-tobacco, the usual reference index for euro area inflation swaps) trades on a fixed-base convention. This implies that for any given day during the settlement month the base equals the lagged reference index value, with a three-month lag for HICPx swaps. For a 10y ILS entered on May 11, 2021, for example, the starting reference index for every trading day during the month equals the February 2021 HICPx print of 105.10.

This facilitates the valuation of ILS during the same calendar month, as the reference index value and therefore the final cash-flows are equal. In addition, the "carry" arising from rolling into the next base month can be quantified, as due to the lagged indexation HICPx values are known for up to 3.5 months ahead.

French and US ILS in contrast trade on an interpolated base convention, with the daily reference index computed in similar fashion as on the cash market (see Chapter 1).

Linker Asset Swaps: The Link Between Cash and Derivative Markets

Via inflation swaps, index-linked bonds (ILBs) can also be converted into nominal ones. All future cash-flows of an inflation-linked bond are by definition unknown ex-ante as they are linked to realized inflation in the future. Using inflation swaps, however, we can transfer these cash-flows into an ex-ante known cash-flow by receiving fixed and paying out the inflation-linked component we receive on the bond. This enables market participants to asset-swap inflation-linked bonds. Asset-swapping also forms the crucial link between cash and derivative inflation markets.

While directly swapping an unknown cash-flow is not feasible, transferring the index-linked cash-flow into a known cash-flow makes swapping this cash-flow stream as straightforward as is the case for any other ex-ante known cash-flow.

Linker (par–par) asset-swaps work the following way:

1. At inception, the asset swap (ASW) buyer purchases the bond at the prevailing market price in return for a par ILB (PILB). Note that as most ILBs typically trade above par, the counterpart is effectively lending to the ASW-buyer.
2. During the holding period of the trade, the investor pays the ILBs' inflation-linked coupon and receives the spread over Libor on par or PILB (i.e., the ASW-spread). Note that due to the indexation, the notional of the ILB and thus the coupon payment increase in line with the index ratio, while the swap notional is fixed. In line with nominal bonds, the ASW-spread is derived from setting the net present value of all cash-flows of the ASW equal to zero at inception.
3. At maturity, the ASW buyer receives par or PILB and pays the inflation-uplifted principal.

Figure 3.13 highlights the cash-flows and underlying principle of linker asset swaps:

IOTA Spreads

Linker ASW-spreads are a popular tool to assess the relative value of a linker as it removes mechanical biases stemming from seasonality and inflation accruals. In particular, the ASW- (or z-spread) differential between a linker and its nominal comparable measures the richness/cheapness of a linker against the swap curve.

The difference (ASWILB – ASWNominal) is also called IOTA spread,[4] and is typically positive given the lower liquidity of ILBs versus their nominal peers as well as the bullet payment at maturity and hence higher credit risk of ILBs.

4 "Iota" is the unit for Implied Impact. It is measured in basis points (bp) as the spread between the standard risk-adjusted financial return and the impact-adjusted financial return (1 Iota = 1 bp of

Linker asset swaps: a graphical illustration

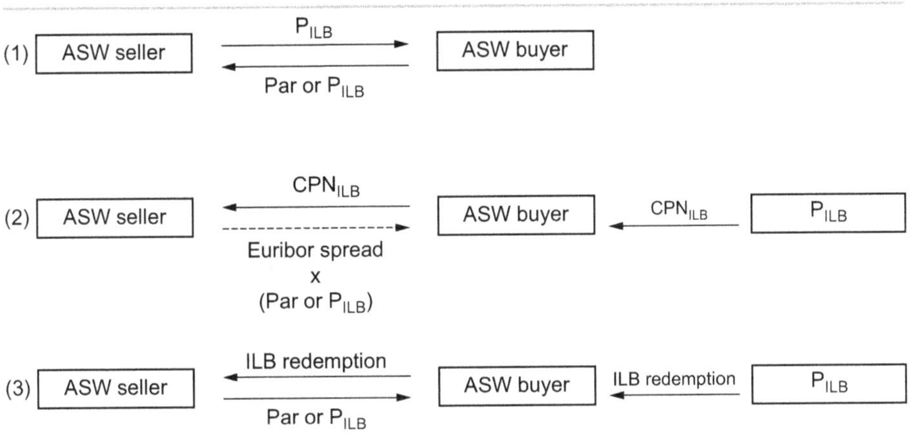

Figure 3.13: Linker Asset Swap cashflows.
Source: Commerzbank Research.

Given the no-arbitrage condition between the cash and derivatives markets, a long break-even position via ILBs (adjusted for seasonality) is economically equivalent to a long position in ILS of the same maturity minus the IOTA-spread (recall that the IOTA spread captures the premium/discount of the ILB versus the swap curve).

Hence, the IOTA spread can be approximated as

$$\text{IOTAILB,t} \approx \text{ILSt} - \text{seasonality-adjusted break-evenILB,t}$$

Figure 3.14 highlights this approximation for the DBRei Apr30, which was issued in April 2014. As can be readily seen, the seasonality-adjusted break-even of the ILB typically trades well aligned with the interpolated ILS most of the time, but still gives rise to a positive IOTA.

For relative value analysis, IOTA spreads are typically combined with forward break-evens, other rich/cheap measures like z-scores and supply considerations in order to provide a comprehensive picture.

Constructing Inflation Curves

Market-implied measures of future inflation provide a valuable yardstick for putting inflation views into perspective. They form the basis for a wide range of investment and business decisions. Extracting inflation expectations from market instruments is

---

Implied Impact). The inflation Iota spread (linker z-ASW – nominal z-ASW, see p. 34) can be seen as an analytical measure of richness/cheapness of a BE versus inflation swap curve.

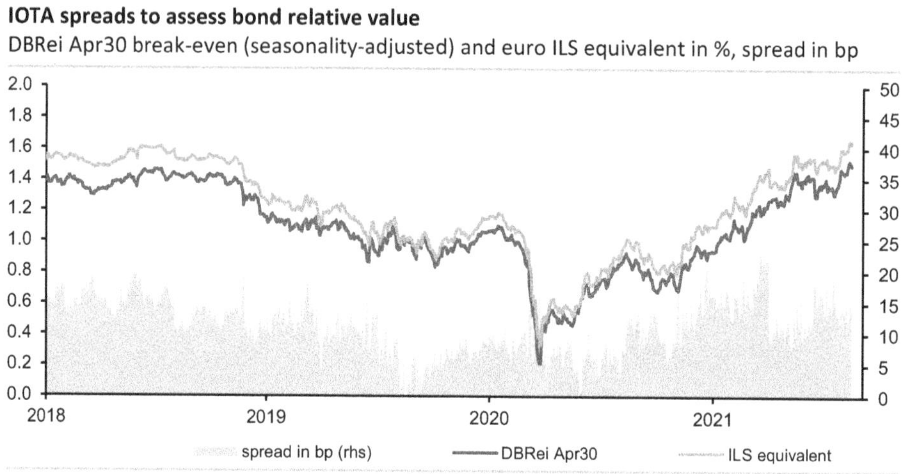

Figure 3.14: IOTA spreads.
Source: Bloomberg, Commerzbank Research.

not without its pitfalls, however. While linker break-evens are prone to giving biased indications of inflation expectations discounted by markets, inflation derivatives mitigate these shortcomings. They also form the building-block for the pricing of other inflation- linked instruments. We therefore provide a comprehensive guide for constructing inflation curves.

Getting a Handle on Market-based Inflation Expectations

Market-implied measures of future inflation provide a valuable yardstick for putting inflation expectations into perspective and form the basis for a wide range of investment and business decisions. Extracting inflation expectations from quoted instruments is not without pitfalls, however.

While the standard measure, that is, the level of linker break-evens, is readily observable, the (il)liquidity and credit premia embedded in inflation linkers as well as the limited amount of outstanding bonds make cash break-evens sensitive to distortions. Inflation-linked bonds are thus prone to giving biased indications of inflation expectations discounted by the market (see also Chapter 5).

Inflation derivatives mitigate these shortcomings and represent the building-block for the pricing of other inflation-linked instruments, to uncover trading opportunities as well as the marking-to-market of existing inflation positions. We therefore provide a comprehensive guide for constructing spot and forward inflation curves.

From Inflation Swaps to Forward HICPx and ILS Rates

Zero coupon inflation-linked swaps (ILS) on HICPx (Harmonised Index of Consumer Prices ex-tobacco) form the starting point for constructing inflation curves, as we see in Figure 3.15. They offer good liquidity and are actively traded across a wide range of maturities. By construction the quoted ILS rate represents the average annual inflation expected over the term of the swap. Stripping out future inflation levels and annual forward rates is therefore straightforward.

Compounding the spot rate over the term of the swap generates the projected reference index value (RefCPI) at the maturity date:

$$RefCPI_t = (1 + ILS_t)^t \times RefCPI_{Settle} \tag{1}$$

The other central ingredient is the annual forward inflation rate ($fwdILS_t$), which denotes the constant growth rate of inflation between two annual points. Following standard market practice we assume $fwdILS_t$ are piece-wise continuous and given by:

$$fwdILS_t = \ln(RefCPI_{t+1}) - \ln(RefCPI_t) \tag{2}$$

The building block for constructing inflation curves: from zero coupon Inflation swap rates to future reference index levels

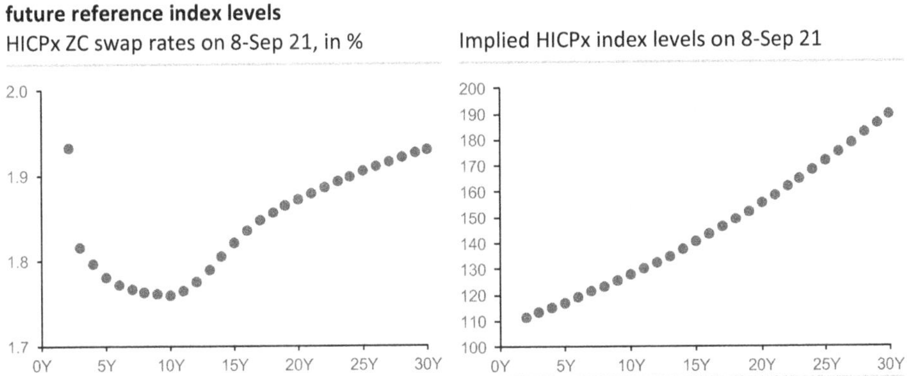

Figure 3.15: Inflation index levels and zero coupon swaps.
Source: Bloomberg, Commerzbank Research

The Devil's in the Detail: Accounting for Seasonality

These forward index ratios and rates apply to the respective settlement month only. For practical purposes, like the valuation of derivatives or the computation of linker ASW-spreads, however, reference values for intermediate months (or days) are typically required.

Linearly extrapolating the constant forward inflation rate between two annual points on the ILS curve represents an intuitive approach for obtaining monthly reference index projections. The index level m months and t years after the settlement date is given by:

$$RefCPI_{m,t} = RefCPI_t \times e^{fwdILS \times m/12} \tag{3}$$

However, this approach implicitly assumes a constant inflation rate throughout the year. In other words, linear interpolation ignores the seasonality of inflation indices (see the right-hand chart of Figure 3.16).

Recall that ILS are tied to non-seasonally adjusted price series and therefore exhibit substantial monthly swings over the course of the year. Well-known examples are the prices for clothing and package tourism, which significantly impact the reference index (as we will discuss in Chapter 5). Accounting for seasonality is therefore crucial to obtain correct monthly (and daily) reference index values, and thus inflation curves. Therefore, the interpolated reference index projection requires adjustments.

How exactly is this achieved? Given seasonal adjustment factors for the reference index and assuming that these remain constant over time enables us to compute the adjusted index levels for any given month between two annual points on the curve.

First, the seasonal adjustment for the settlement month is zero. As monthly seasonal effects feed through the entire year, the seasonal adjustment for the m'th month thereafter is given by the sum of the m seasonal contributions after the settlement month. Note also that by definition the seasonal factors sum up to zero, that is, there is no seasonal effect in YoY terms. The seasonal adjustment (SA) is then applied to the linearly interpolated reference index value of the month in question (in technical terms, the inflation rate is decomposed into a trend and a seasonal factor):

$$\text{adjusted}\, RefCPI_{m,t} = RefCPI_{m,t} \times e^{SA} \tag{4}$$

The following example illustrates this concept for HICPx swaps. The reference fixing for 8-Sep 2021 is June 1 (recall that index values are applied with a 3m lag with ILS trading on a fixed base convention, i.e., for any given day during the settlement month the starting reference index equals the 3m lagged HICPx). The HICPx values for June 2026 and June 2027 implied by the spot ILS curve are 117.13 and 119.16, respectively. The average annual inflation rate between June 2026 and June 2027 thus equals 1.72 percent [ln(119.16)-ln(117.13)]. For a given month between those dates, say November 2026, interpolation is required and applying formula (3) delivers an unadjusted HICPx value of 117.97.

The seasonal adjustment is obtained by summing up the seasonal adjustments from June to November, which in our example amounts to -0.38 percent. The last step is computing the adjusted HICPx projection, which equals 117.52, with a corresponding ZC ILS rate of 1.58 percent. This deviates 7bp from the unadjusted rate of 1.65 percent, and distortions can be even more pronounced for shorter maturities given the inverse relationship with duration (see Figure 3.16). Incorporating seasonality is therefore imperative.

Seasonality-adjusted versus unadjusted CPI levels and forward rates

Interpolated HICPx forward curve on 8-Sep 21 | Interpolated 1y forward euro ILS rates*, in %

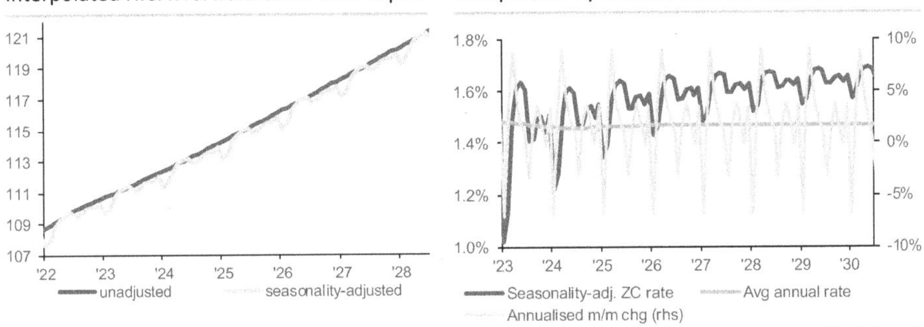

Figure 3.16: Seasonality and interpolation in CPI.
Source: Bloomberg, Commerzbank Research, *) from seasonality-adjusted HICPx forward curve.

Completing the Puzzle: Seasonality-Adjusted CPI Curves

Once the adjusted reference index levels have been computed, the projected break-even rate for the month can be readily extracted (see equation 1). In addition, having obtained the monthly reference values, future daily reference values can be computed in similar fashion as for inflation-linked bonds.

Applying this technique to the CPI and ILS term structures results in an oscillating pattern between any two annual points on the curve, as can be seen in Figures 3.16 and 3.17. The same holds true for interpolated annualized forward inflation rates (see the right-hand chart of Figure 3.16). Note that the intra-year rate can also be above the longer tenor (e.g., the 3.5y is larger than the 3y rate), which is somewhat counterintuitive. The substantial difference again underscores the need to adjust for seasonality, in particular for shorter maturities.

The magnitude of the seasonal distortion weakens over time. This arises from the fact that seasonality is zero in YoY terms, while ILS are annualized rates and the monthly seasonality impact hence mechanically smoothens out over time.

These techniques can also be applied to ILS trading on an interpolated base convention, like the French and US inflation market. On these the reference index value is computed by interpolating between the m-2 and m-3 reference index value, similarly as on the cash market. Rather than being fixed for the whole month as for markets trading on a fixed base convention (like HICPx, see above), the starting reference index value therefore differs for every day of the settlement month. The computation of seasonal effects is therefore slightly more complicated, as it may encompass partial months.

Oscillating inflation curves highlight the need to incorporate seasonality
HICPx ZC ILS curve on 8-Sep-21, in %

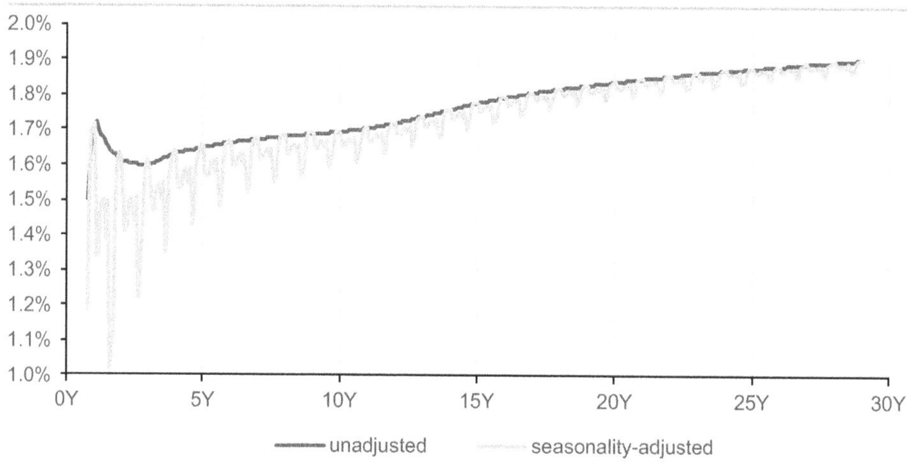

Figure 3.17: Osscillatory patterns in inflation seasonality.
Source: Eurostat, Bloomberg, Commerzbank Research.

For horizons below one year, monthly CPI levels derived via seasonal adjustments need to be treated with some caution. For such short horizons, the individual seasonal factors have an exponential impact on the implied index levels. At the same time, there is no common market standard for estimating seasonal factors and in any case the expected m/m change may deviate from the seasonal profile. To control for these factors, inflation markets use broker fixings as the benchmark for sub-1y inflation expectations (i.e., the month-on-month profile for the coming twelve months). These broker-based forwards allow trading the expected fixing of the CPI index for a given month. Give their comparatively high liquidity, they hence deliver robust and directly observable market-based expectations for the y/y (or m/m) rates.

Following Covid-19 and its impact on consumption patterns and delivery chains, the deviations between the seasonality-implied and broker-based inflation expectations have become pronounced. The January 2022 HICPx release provides the most prominent example: while the January seasonal adjustment (as well as most economists) argued for a m/m decline, broker-based expectations were anticipating a flat change as well as repeated deviations from the seasonal pattern throughout the year, probably reflecting the deviations already observable throughout 2021 (see Figure 3.18).

Broker-based forwards the benchmark for horizons below one year
Month-on-month change of euro HICPx, ILS-based/broker-based forecasts, HICP seasonal, in %

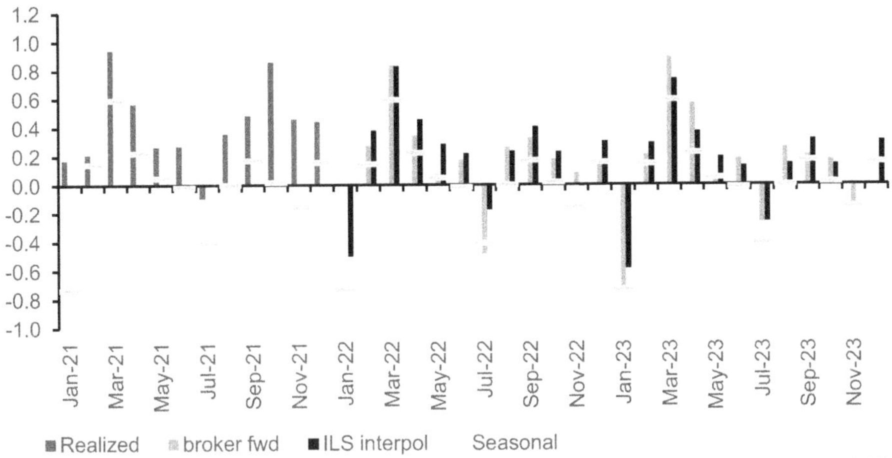

Figure 3.18: Broker-based vs interpolated and seasonality adjusted forwards.
Source: Eurostat, Bloomberg, Commerzbank Research.

Chapter 4
Forwards, Carry and Trading Strategies

Carry is a concept that crops up all over the financial markets. It refers to systematic differences between points on a curve, be that inflation, bond rates or options. Perhaps one of the oldest examples is simple interest rate carry. On average, interest rates rise with the tenor of the investment or borrowing. Thus, if a long-term investment is funded by rolling short-term borrowings, this can generate a profit in the long term. More generally carry now refers to this type of tenor-related effect over many different curve types. Carry effects can substantially impact the return profile of index-linked products and a good understanding of how it pertains to these products is therefore crucial for positioning in linker space.

Carry Computation

Calculating forwards and the carry of inflation-linked bonds (ILB) is a different process than the calculation for their nominal peers: in addition to the coupons, ILBs also generate income via the inflation accrual. Hence, future CPI readings drive the carry of linkers as well as their forwards.

The underlying idea for computing forward prices for inflation-linked bonds and their nominal counterparts is the same. To calculate forward prices and carry, one has to compare the income derived from a given asset with the costs of funding the position. "No arbitrage" prescribes that the forward price of any asset equals the spot price plus the financing costs minus the income generated. For fixed income assets, this income equals the coupon accrual. If the income generated exceeds the costs of funding, forward prices will be below spot and the asset has positive carry.

Inflation Accrual Complicates Carry Calculation

There is one complicating factor for inflation-linked bonds: in addition to the real coupon, linkers also generate income via the change in the CPI between the settlement and the horizon date – that is, the inflation accrual. Forward prices and thus carry are to a large extent determined by these changes in CPI readings. The following formulas help to illustrate the underlying concept:

(1) Forward Price = Spot Price + Repo Costs – Income

(2) Income = Real Coupon Accrual + Inflation Accrual

(3) Carry = Real Forward Yield – Real Spot Yield

https://doi.org/10.1515/9783110787429-004

Positive Inflation Implies Positive Carry for Linkers

Linker forward prices are to a large extent determined by the inflation accrual, that is, the growth of the index ratio (IR) between the settlement and the horizon date. Assuming that the IR grows (i.e., $IR_{FWD} > IR_{Spot}$), the real forward price will fall. This implies that the spot price can drop to the forward price over the holding period before the position starts losing money. The inflation accrual compensates for the drop in real prices by increasing prices again in nominal space.

In that case, the real forward yield is above the real spot yield and the ILB has positive carry (see equation 3).

The reverse holds if the IR declines over the period in question. In the case of a negative inflation accrual, the forward price could even be higher than the spot price and the real forward yield would accordingly be lower than spot yield.

The right-hand chart in Figure 4.1 exemplifies such a scenario via the 1m forward real yield for the DBRei Apr30 on August 18, 2021, assuming different Jul-21 HICPx readings and funding at 6bp below the Euro OverNight Index Average (EONIA). Remember that the July HICPx is used as a reference index for October (see Chapter 2; the actual interpolated figure is 107.13 resulting in negative carry of 0.9bp).

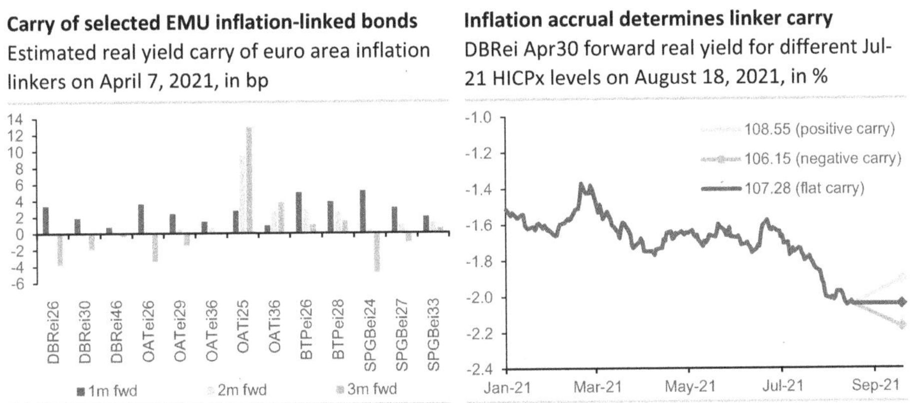

Figure 4.1: ILB carry and inflation accrual.
Source: Bloomberg, Commerzbank Research.

Carry, Forward-spreads and Trading Strategies

Carry can significantly impact the total return of index-linked products and is a key factor for trading strategies in inflation products. We can extend the carry concepts from the previous section to calculate the carry for nominal bonds – and thus the carry for break-even positions, that is, break-even carry.

In line with the break-even definition outlined in Chapter 2, break-even carry is the difference between the carry of the nominal equivalent and the carry of the corresponding linker.

Carry Impact on Break-even Positions

Negative break-even carry hence indicates that it is advantageous to hold a linker rather than the nominal counterpart over a specific time horizon. Break-even carry also shows the amount in basis points the break-even rate can fall without the position incurring a loss (see the left-hand chart in Figure 4.2).

This typically applies during periods of positive inflation accruals, that is, a rising index ratio, which will be applied to the ILB's principal (and coupon). Conversely, nominals are more attractive from a carry point of view in the case of positive break-even carry, with the latter indicating how much break-evens have to rise for the position to "break-even."

A key point is that carry of index-linked bonds – that is, real rate carry – is significantly larger, can be sharply negative and is also much more volatile than the carry of conventional coupon bonds (see the right-hand chart of Figure 4.2). This is due to the seasonality of price indices and thus heavily varying inflation accruals month-on-month (we will provide an in-depth discussion of seasonality in Chapter 5).

Accordingly, the carry of break-even positions is primarily driven by the inflation accrual.

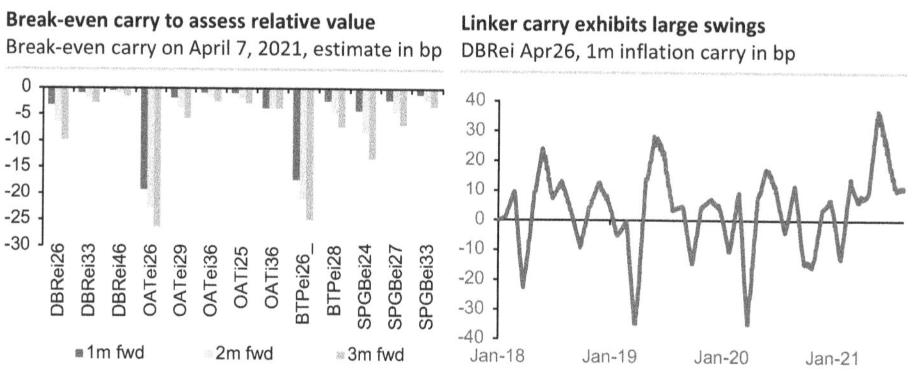

Figure 4.2: Break-even linker carry.
Source: Bloomberg, Commerzbank Research.

Measuring the Carry Contribution

Carry can significantly bias the dynamics of inflation-linked bonds. Falling (unadjusted) real yields between two points in time might be driven entirely by large carry during the period, rather than changes in economic or market prospects; all else being equal, a higher unadjusted clean price has to balance the falling value of the inflation accrual approaching the forward date. The very negative January seasonal effect represents the most prominent example.

Focusing on the spot level of break-evens and real yields can thus give misleading signals regarding the richness or cheapness of an ILB. Low (and/or falling) spot break-evens, for example, can simply reflect a negative inflation accrual (that is, lagged seasonality). In such a case, including forward break-evens is important to assess the risk/reward.

Carry is therefore a key factor to consider as it can significantly impact the total return of trading strategies in inflation products. Figure 4.3 highlights the crucial impact of carry via unadjusted and carry-adjusted break-evens. The divergence between both measures over shorter and longer time periods can be profound.

For a long break-even position in the DBRei Apr26 entered on January 1, 2020 and held until August 19, 2021 for example, linker carry has contributed 43bp to the total return of 82bp. In addition, the unadjusted break-even rate also would have missed the negative carry contribution at the height of the Covid-19 pandemic (see Figure 4.3).

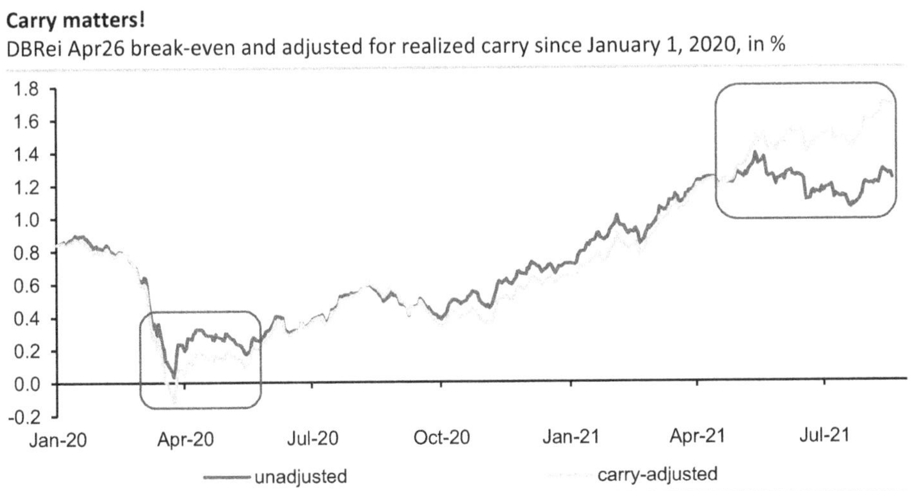

Figure 4.3: Adjusting for carry.
Source: Bloomberg, Commerzbank Research.

Using Forward-spreads for Break-even Trades

Isolating inflation accruals from genuine real yield changes is therefore important in order to interpret linker dynamics. This applies in particular for total return analysis and relative value trading decisions and can be achieved by converting the inflation accrual accumulated during the holding period into basis points, via the analytical techniques discussed in this chapter.

Implied forward break-evens and spreads allow us to quickly evaluate the impact of carry on a given trading strategy.

An example: Figure 4.4 shows that the forward break-even of the DBRei Apr26 on August 19, 2021 is above the spot level, by 7.3bp on a 2m horizon, in essence reflecting the negative real yield carry of the ILB (8.4bp). In other words, if the break-even rate rises more than 7.3bp, long positions generate a profit. Note also that the 3m forward break-even is at the upper end of the trading range, indicating that a substantial move would be required for the position to generate positive return.

That being said, inflation markets typically price value swings very efficiently in the carry profile. During periods of high positive carry (for example in May when the very positive March seasonal effect kicks in), the ILB's clean price tends to remain stable while a gradually higher real yield balances the rising inflation accrual as the spot date rolls into the forward date.

Forward break-evens to evaluate richness/cheapness

DBRei Apr26 and Apr30 break-even rate and implied forwards, on August 19, 2021 in %

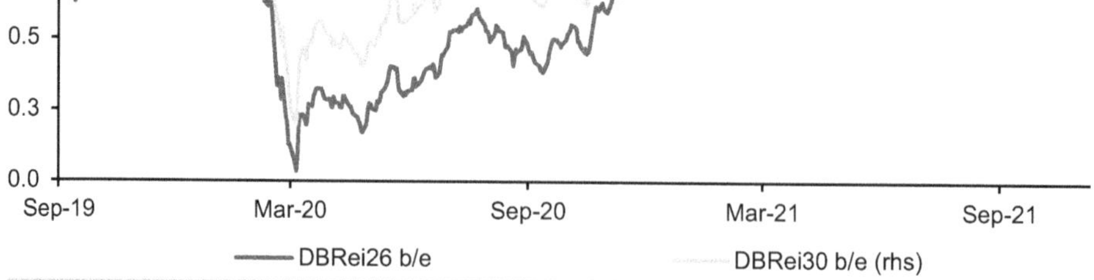

Figure 4.4: Forward break-evens.
Source: Bloomberg, Commerzbank Research.

Carry Versus Seasonal Adjustments

Regarding (nominal-equivalent) total return, carry-adjusted break-evens provide the cleanest measure as they take the evolution of the CPI index since the settlement date into account, in contrast to seasonality-adjusted break-evens (and/or real yields). Seasonality adjustments are entirely determined by the balance of seasonal effects of the ILB‘s cash-flow date and the settlement date of the position – that is, they have no “memory” and both seasonal effects are fixed across calendar years (see Chapter 5). Carry adjustments in contrast depend on the progression of the index ratio since the position was opened (the settlement date).

Accordingly, realized carry is a fact while seasonal adjustments are subject to model risk as the seasonal factor for a given month has to be estimated and can over/understate the relevant month-on-month changes that will eventually be realized.

Figure 4.5 highlights the difference between unadjusted, seasonality-adjusted and carry-adjusted break-evens for the DBRei Apr26 (with reference date April 15, 2020). As is clearly visible, seasonality-adjusted break-evens would understate the total return as they do not include the large accumulated real yield carry.

Once more, the difference between these measures increases with the absolute difference between the settlement and cash-flow month of the ILB as the seasonality adjustment converges to zero approaching the cash-flow date. It also mechanically increases when evaluating time horizons of more than one year.

Assessing total linker return

DBRei Apr26 break-even and adjusted for seasonality and cumulated carry since January 1, 2020, in %

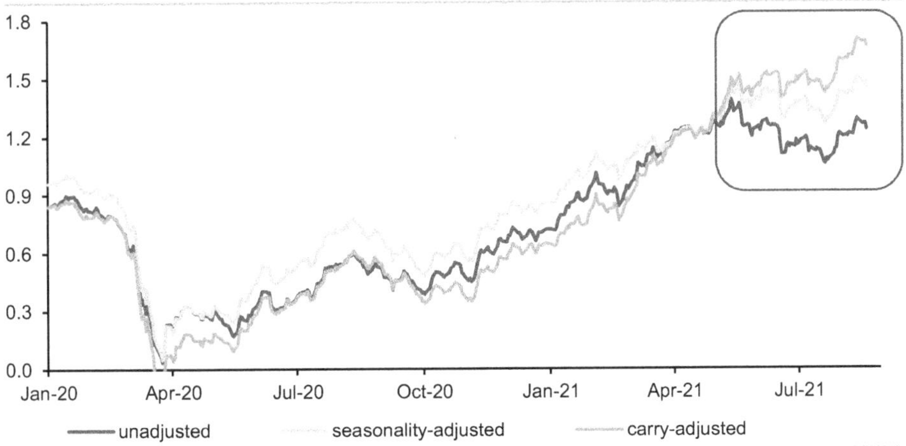

Figure 4.5: Total linker return.
Source: Bloomberg, Commerzbank Research.

Carry Impact on Curve Positions

The implications for curve positions are equally important. During periods of positive inflation accruals, real yield steepeners and break-even curve flatteners offer positive carry.

The explanation for that is as follows: In percentage terms, the inflation accrual is identical for all bonds tied to the same reference index. Apart from level effects due to differences in prices, this also implies that all bonds across the curve accrue approximately the same absolute inflation compensation.

However, an investor has to buy a greater nominal amount of short-dated bonds than of long-dated bonds in curve positions in order to obtain the same delta. To phrase it differently, 1 percent of inflation accrual does not translate into the same amount of yield shift owing to varying durations along the curve. This also explains why carry on short-dated ILBs is much more sensitive to changes in the index ratio compared to longer-dated linkers.

As discussed earlier, forward real yields are above spot yields if inflation-linked bonds have positive carry. This in turn offers protection against rising real yields. However, the magnitude by which forward yields are above spot will be significantly larger at the front-end of the curve than at the long end.

A 1 percent rise in the price of a 5y bond has a stronger impact on the 5y bond's yield than a 1 percent rise has for a 30y bond. In a positive carry environment, real yield curve steepeners – that is, buying a short dated ILB and selling a long dated one – have positive carry, and the forward curve is thus flatter than the spot curve (higher front-end carry versus long-end carry).

Carry Impact on Break-even Box Trades

The carry profile is the opposite for break-even curves. Remember, the break-evens represent a spread between nominal and real yields. A break-even curve spread is therefore a spread between two break-even rates, and hence a box trade between nominals and linkers. The carry of nominals is unaffected by inflation accruals, while real yield carry is typically substantial as explained above.

In a 5–30y break-even curve flattener (Figure 4.6), we look for 5y break-evens to outperform 30y break- evens. We are thus long 30y nominals versus linkers and simultaneously long 5y linkers versus nominals. This is equivalent to holding a steepener on the real yield curve versus a flattener on the nominal curve (see Figure 4.6). Positive linker carry implies that the real yield steepener has positive carry as explained before, leaving the break-even flattener with positive carry overall (for simplicity's sake, we assume flat carry on nominals in this example).

Having derived break-even carry, we can easily compute the carry on break-even flatteners. What about the carry of a 5–10y break-even flattener on the German curve over a 1m horizon, for example?

The DBRei Apr26 has a break-even carry of 7.2bp and the DBRei Apr30 4.1bp for settlement on 19-Aug 2021 (i.e., both ILBs carry worse than their nominal peers, due to the negative carry environment). To make the position delta-neutral, we have to buy 49 percent of the DBRei Apr30 break-even for every cent of DBRei Apr26 break-even, resulting in a negative carry for the break-even curve flattener of 3.1bp.

The latter also provides the implied 1m forward break-even curve-spread. Putting forward spreads in context of the curve's history also allows us to quickly evaluate the carry-impact and attractiveness of a break-even curve trade.

Break-even curve trades
Break-even curve flattener = flattener in nominals and steepener in linkers

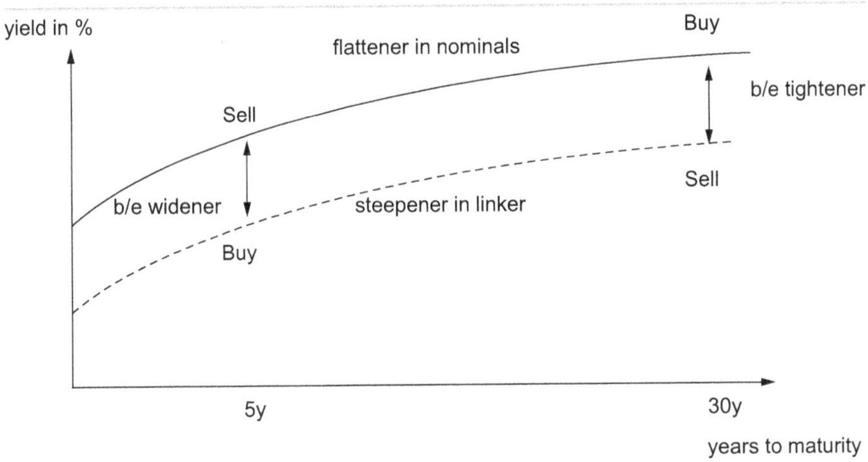

Figure 4.6: Break-even curve trades.
Source: Commerzbank Research.

Chapter 5
Inflation Expectations, Seasonality and Base Effects

Decoding Market-based Inflation Expectations

Where do people think that inflation will go? Up, down, static? While we can extract forward inflation prices from the inflation products, does this actually reflect genuine inflation expectations? And how do we account for the seasonal effects embedded in consumer price indices, like post-Christmas sales or July reductions in the retail sector? Relying on one measure only can be misleading given the various structural and mechanical pitfalls of inflation products. In this chapter, we present a broader set of metrics and cross-checks in order to obtain a robust and comprehensive picture of market-based inflation expectations. As former European Central Bank (ECB) president Mario Draghi has said, "observing the universe" of inflation markets is crucial, as are cross-checks with survey-based measures for longer-dated inflation expectations.[1]

What to Look at?

The 5-year inflation average in 5 years' time (5y5y inflation-linked swap or ILS) is a popular measure of market-implied inflation expectations, not least because the underlying spot rates constitute by far most actively traded points on the euro area and the US inflation swap curves (see Chapter 3). Like any other forward, 5y5y ILS rates primarily reflect the steepness of the inflation swap curve, and they are entirely determined by the 5y and 10y ILS spot rates. Changes in the 5–10y curve dynamic hence have to be monitored closely, as isolated moves in 5y and 10y ILS rather than changes in genuine inflation expectations can explain sharp moves in forward space.

The 5y5y euro ILS are typically closely correlated to the 5y spot rate, but this correlation can break down materially. In February 2015, for example, the 5–10y ILS curve was trading more than 2 standard deviations below the levels implied by outright ILS following the very aggressive curve flattening since the start of that year.

In addition, the drift of ILS can render historical comparisons misleading. For example, a 4y1y HICPx forward entered in August 2021 captures the expected y/y

1 https://www.washingtonpost.com/news/wonk/wp/2014/08/27/can-mario-draghi-save-the-euro-again/.

https://doi.org/10.1515/9783110787429-005

HICPx inflation in May 2026, while six months prior the same forward reflected the expectation for December 2025 – which can be very severely distorted by the seasonality of inflation indices (which are discussed in detail later in this chapter).

Year-end HICPx Helps to Obtain a Comprehensive Picture

To address these pitfalls, we can focus on the dynamics of year-end HICPx implied by inflation swaps. In other words, we assess how the market price for the y/y HICPx rate in December in each of the coming years has evolved over time (see Figure 5.1). This measure takes into account the full ILS term structure and hence provides a comprehensive picture across time horizons.

By computing the implied price of HICPx for fixed-time horizons we also circumvent various pitfalls in interpreting inflation curves discussed above.

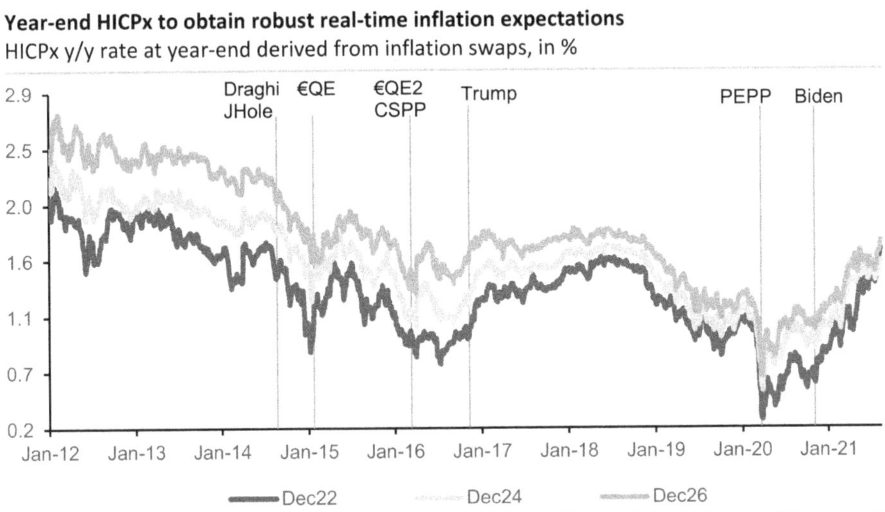

Figure 5.1: Inflation expectations derived from inflation swaps.
Source: Bloomberg, Commerzbank Research.

Assessing the Full CPI Curve

This approach is particularly relevant for drawing historical comparisons and analysing the impact of events like verbal central bank interventions, HICP releases or the pandemic.

Crucially, it takes into account the whole inflation curve, which is particularly useful for assessing spillovers into longer-dated inflation expectations, for example arising from commodity price declines or weak core inflation prints. Implied year-end HICPx rates hence deliver a more precise picture of the real-time dynamics in inflation expectations.

A Few Examples

Figure 5.1 highlights the large impact of the announcement of €QE in January 2015. While neither Draghi's unexpected change of script in Jackson Hole in August 2014, nor his observation that market-based inflation expectations were "excessively low" thereafter could turn around inflation expectations on a sustained basis, Euro QE reversed the massive decline of Dec-22 HICPx. Most important, it stopped the accelerating decline in longer maturities, that is, the substantial spillover of collapsing commodity prices that suggested a de-anchoring of inflation expectations during that period.

A similar impact is observable after the ECB's decision to raise the monthly Euro QE volume to €80bn alongside the introduction of the CSPP, which stabilized longer horizons.

During the pandemic, the immediate horizons were most affected with Dec22 HICPx for example dropping close to zero as deflation fears moved centre stage. The various policy initiatives by the ECB and EU and in particular the rapidly improving US growth prospects in the wake of Biden's election pushed year-end HICPx to multi-year highs across time horizons as 2021 drew to a close.

Cross-checks to Complete the Picture

Asset Swap (ASW) Spreads

The cash linker market provides another yardstick. While relative asset swap spreads (i.e., the spread between a linker and its nominal peer in ASW-terms) can fluctuate, seasonality-adjusted linker break-evens and the corresponding ILS rate typically move closely in sync. Deviations between ILS and longer-dated (seasonality-adjusted) cash break-evens can thus serve as a warning sign (see Figure 5.2).

ILS Versus SPF

Survey-based measures for inflation expectations like the 5y ahead level mean the inflation estimates of the Society of Professional Forecasters (SPF) are another benchmark for assessing dynamics in ILS (see Figure 5.3). These measures also control for swings in the (il)liquidity and inflation risk premium of inflation-linked products, which can materially distort the "true" underlying inflation expectations of index-linked products.

ILBs versus ILS
DBRei Apr30 break-even (seasonality-adjusted) and Euro ILS equivalent in %, spread in bp

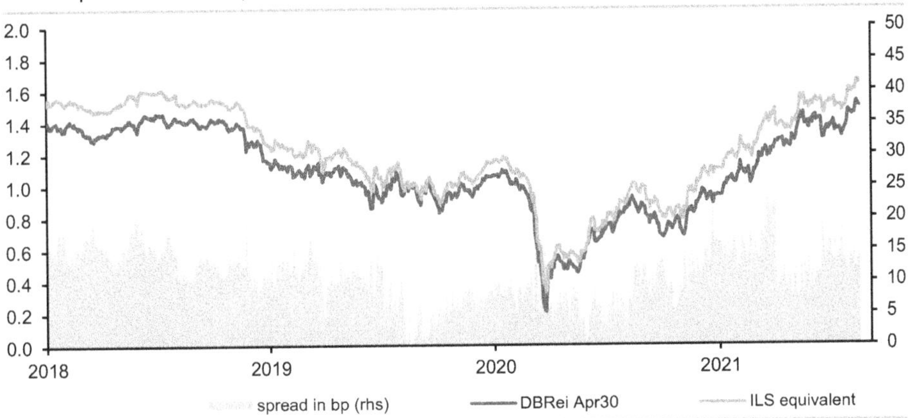

Figure 5.2: ILB vs ILS with spread.
Source: Bloomberg, Commerzbank Research.

Market versus survey-based measures
5y5y Euro ILS and true mean* of 5y ahead inflation expectation of the ECB Survey of Professional Forecasters (SPF), in %

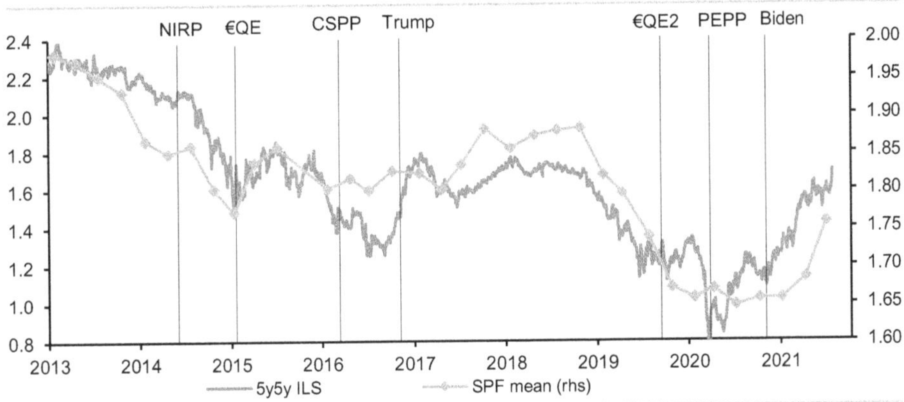

Figure 5.3: Market vs survey based inflation expectations.
Source: Bloomberg, Commerzbank Research, * average of individual forecasts adjusted for outliers.

That being said, SPF expectations are typically only available with a significant time lag of up to three months. Thus, changes in ILS can only be attributed retrospectively to changing risk/liquidity premia. In addition, day-to-day volatility between two SPF points can only be benchmarked against an interpolated SPF value.

Market Versus ECB/SMA Expectations

The ECB's staff projections as well as the Survey of Monetary Analysts (SMA) conducted by the ECB are other benchmarks for market-based inflation expectations. The ECB projections and SMA deliver median expectations for annual average inflation rates for the coming years. In addition, they also provide more granular quarterly profiles. Both measures can be compared to the (interpolated and seasonality-adjusted) HICPx levels implied by the spot ILS curve (for details on constructing CPI curves, see chapter 3).

Figures 5.4 and 5.5 highlight that in the July 2021 SMA, market-based expectations were well aligned with the ECB and monetary analysts with quarterly rates progressing in a synchronised manner. Note that broker-based forwards are used for time horizons below two years (for details see Chapter 3).

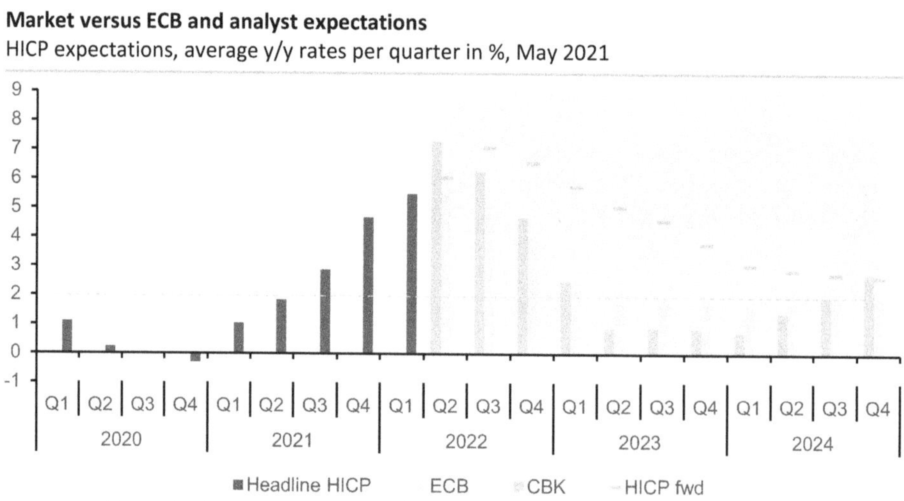

Figure 5.4: Market vs ECB expectations.
Source: Bloomberg, Commerzbank Research.

Regarding long-run expectations, markets at the time were more pessimistic than analysts, which was probably due to presence of risk and (il)liquidity as described above. Note that the ECB does not provide a long-run inflation expectation.

Option-implied Expectations

Identifying the underlying drivers of break-even changes is important. Inflation risks are often driven not by inflation uncertainty as such but by the balance of inflation risks, in particular regarding the tails of the probability distribution (i.e., deflation versus high inflation).

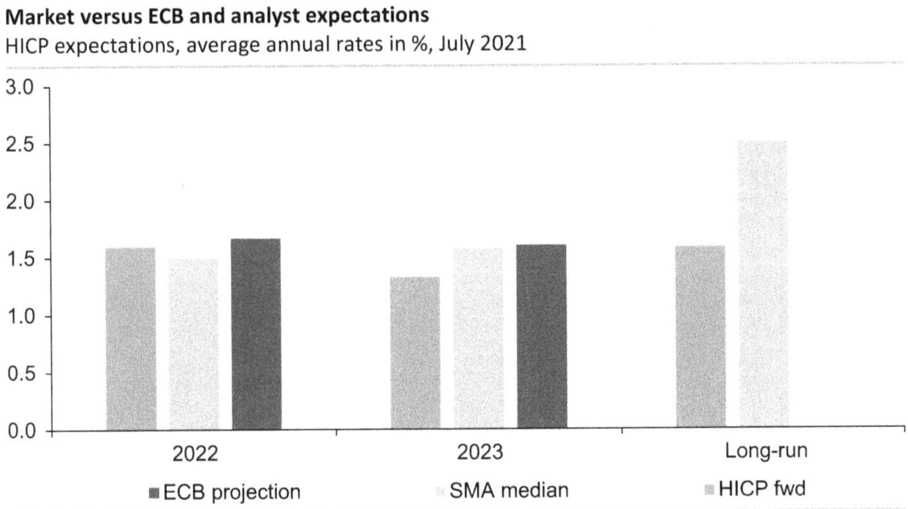

Figure 5.5: Market, median and analyst inflation expectations.
Source: Bloomberg, Commerzbank Research.

In theory, the inflation risk premium (IRP) can hence be captured via shifts across the probability distribution of future inflation (for details see also Chapter 7). To that end, option-implied inflation expectations derived from HICPx cap and floor quotes can deliver valuable information, as they allow us to capture the interaction of inflation tail risks as perceived by the market, and in real time.

However, in practice care has to be applied when interpreting the results as the option-implied probability distributions suspiciously resemble a normal distribution and thus do not deliver genuine information about the tails but rather constitute a fitting exercise (for an in-depth discussion see Chapter 7).

This being said, deflation floors for HICPx have delivered comparatively robust pricing signals given the deflation floor embedded in Euro-area linkers (see Chapter 2). At the same time, deflation has been the major tail risks for Euro linkers until late 2021 given the protracted "low growth, low inflation" environment from 2014 up to that time.

Accordingly, changing deflation/inflation expectations have repeatedly emerged as the key driver for 5y5y Euro ILS, as can be seen in Figure 5.6.

Seasonality De-mystified

While inflation-linked products should primarily reflect market expectations of future inflation, seasonality can significantly distort their break-even rates. Getting a handle on seasonality is thus crucial to obtain unbiased measures of the market's inflation expectation as well as for positioning in linker space.

Euro deflation expectations can tip the balance

Option-implied Euro deflation expectations from 5y HICPx caps/floors and 5y5y € ILS, in %

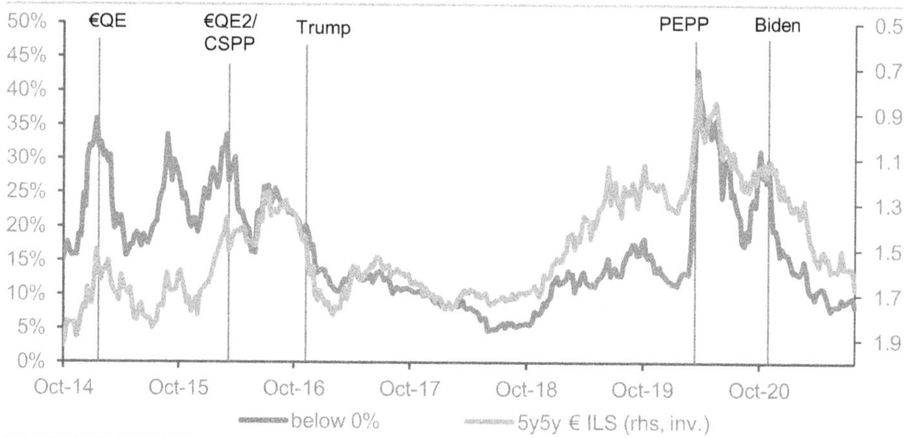

Figure 5.6: Option implied Euro area deflation expectations.
Source: Bloomberg, Commerzbank Research.

What is Seasonality and Where Does it Come From?

Consumer Prices Fluctuate Throughout the Year

Inflation-linked bonds and swaps are tied to non-seasonally adjusted price series. These price indices are derived from aggregating the underlying components of their respective basket of consumer goods, which exhibit substantial swings over the course of the year. As a consequence, the CPI does not progress smoothly over time but exhibits recurring and predictable deviations from the underlying trend inflation rate. These deviations are known as seasonality or seasonality effects.

Prominent examples are the prices for clothing and packaged tourism. The price decline for clothing typically observable in January on the back of post-Christmas reductions as well as a similar effect in July due to summer sales triggers the retreat of the overall HICP for the euro area.

Figure 5.7 illustrates the seasonality effects for the HICPx and the crucial impact of the underlying components.

How Can We Measure Seasonality?

Decomposing the CPI series into a trend, seasonal and noise component allows us to get a handle on seasonality and to quantify its impact. A wide range of statistical tools is available to estimate the monthly seasonal effects, ranging from hands-on moving average (MA) and dummy models to rather complex X-12-ARIMA models. While the latter are the preferred tool of statistics offices, we prefer the MA and dummy models for practical purposes given their flexibility and ease of implementation. Furthermore, ARIMA models are not without theoretical drawbacks.

Seasonality at work: Pronounced swings in CPIs as underlying components fluctuate

HICPx, with/without seasonality adjustment — Weighted contribution to monthly HICPx changes, in %

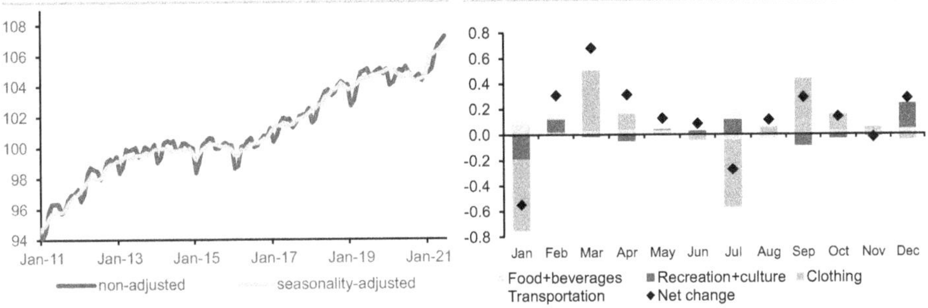

Figure 5.7: Seasonality effects in HICPx.
Source: Eurostat, Bloomberg, Commerzbank Research.

Estimating the dummy model of seasonality is straightforward and can be computed via a spreadsheet. For this the data is regrouped into monthly changes of the CPI index and a monthly dummy is variable added. This allows us to estimate the following equation via Ordinary Least Squares (OLS):

$$\mathrm{CPI}_t = \sum \mathrm{dummy}_t \times \beta_t + \in_t \tag{1}$$

The betas of this regression represent the average inflation for the respective month. Subtracting the average of all betas – which can be interpreted as an annual trend factor – from each single one delivers the seasonal effects. As can be seen on the left-hand chart in Figure 5.8, the seasonal effects for HICPx generated by the dummy model are very similar to those obtained from an X-12-ARIMA model[2]1, underscoring the reliability of the dummy approach for practical purposes.

2 The X-12-ARIMA seasonal effects can be extracted from the adjusted HICPx series published by Eurostat.

Seasonality Impact Differs Across CPIs

Comparing the seasonal effects for HICPx and FRIx reveals that although the general seasonal pattern is similar, the extent is typically different. Changes in tourism prices, for instance, are significantly larger in Germany and also have a substantially higher weight compared to France. As Germany determines roughly 30 percent of the overall euro area index, seasonal swings due to tourism prices can be more pronounced in the European than in the French index.

Care has to be applied with regard to the stability of seasonal estimates over time. As the right-hand chart in Figure 5.8 shows, the impact of seasonality exhibits a pronounced upward trend. In addition, HICP construction methods evolve as the EU commission strives to enhance the reliability and transparency of the index. Revisions or rapidly changing price dynamics of underlying components, like energy prices or pandemic effects, are another source of instability.

Regular re-assessments of the seasonal model and estimates are therefore required.

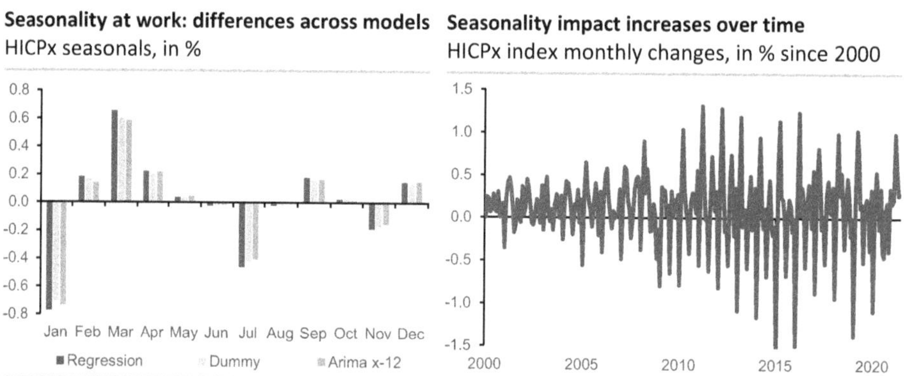

Figure 5.8: Seasonality impact over time.
Source: Eurostat, Bloomberg, Commerzbank Research.

What are the Practical Consequences of Seasonality Effects?

While inflation-linked bonds (ILBs) should primarily reflect market expectations of future inflation (neglecting risk and (il)liquidity for the moment), seasonality can significantly distort the real yields and thus break-evens of ILBs. This is due to the fact that seasonality heavily impacts the inflation accrual and thus the prices of inflation-linked bonds. Recall that monthly CPIs are applied with a three-month time lag. For example, the typical drop in January will take effect from mid-March onwards.[3] Hence, March and April are typically poor carry months for inflation-linked bonds. Similarly, July is usually a strong carry month, given that the monthly change in April tends to be positive.

Seasonality Can Distort Linker Prices

Focusing on the spot level of real yields or break-evens can therefore give misleading signals on the richness or cheapness of an ILB. Historically low break-evens, for example, can simply reflect large negative carry over the coming months – that is, break-evens would have to rise substantially for the position to make a profit.

In addition to these "macro" factors, seasonality also has important ramifications for the relative value of ILBs from different issuers or with different cash-flow dates. German and French linkers are a prominent example. German linkers pay coupons in April, a poor carry month, while French linkers pay coupons and principal in July, thus benefiting from the favorable seasonality profile in the summer. German linkers might thus appear cheap on a break-even basis, but this is merely a reflection of the different seasonality profile of the bonds (see Figure 5.9).

These seasonality distortions decrease with the ILB's maturity and increase with the difference between the settlement and maturity/cash-flow date.

How do Seasonality Adjustments Work?

Adjusting for seasonality is hence crucial for obtaining unbiased measures of the market's inflation expectations. The same is true for isolating mere inflation accruals from genuine real yield changes when analyzing linker returns and positioning in linker space. It is also necessary when comparing bonds with different cash-flow dates, for example for relative value trades or the pricing of new issues in the absence of directly comparable bonds on the issuer's own curve.

Having computed the seasonal effects, we can easily adjust real yields and break-evens. As CPIs show a clear upward trend and the seasonality impact thus feeds through over time, multiplicative seasonal adjustment factors (SAF) are applied to the price of the ILBs. Note also the SAF sum up to zero as there is no seasonality in YoY terms. The next step implies adjusting the quoted ILB price by the respective SAF of the settlement and maturity month. The seasonally adjusted price (SAP) of an ILB is given by the following equation:

3 Due to the calculation method of the daily reference index the January index impacts March inflation accruals.

$$\text{SAP} = P_{ILB} \times \frac{\text{SAF}_{\text{Settle}}}{\text{SAF}_{\text{Maturity}}} \tag{2}$$

The SAP enables us to calculate the adjusted real-yield and break-even of the bond. As is readily visible in the formula above, the seasonality adjustment is essentially a function of the coupon/redemption month of a given bond ($\text{SAF}_{\text{Maturity}}$) with the corresponding seasonal for that month determining both the sign and size of the adjustment.

Note also that the basis point value of the seasonal adjustment falls with duration, that is, it is larger for shorter-dated ILBs.

German Linkers Appear Cheap Versus French Peers Due to Seasonality

Returning to the previous example, the real rate of a German linker implied by its (unadjusted) market price has to be adjusted downward and that of a French linker upward in order to account for the different seasonality profiles. In other words, the break-even of the German linker has to be increased and that of the French linker decreased in order to put the two bonds on an equal footing (see Figure 5.9).

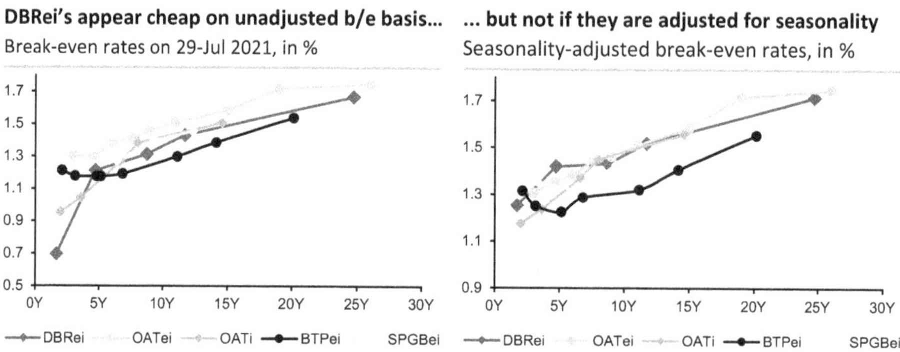

Figure 5.9: Adjusting for Seasonality.
Source: Eurostat, Bloomberg, Commerzbank Research.

In addition to the size of the seasonal adjustment on a given day, the evolution during a given calendar year is also important. Figure 5.10 highlights the estimated seasonal adjustment for Euro linkers with 23s/24s maturities during 2020. In particular for DBRei, this is crucial given the much larger magnitude of the adjustment than for their peers as well as the negative sign that arises from the very negative January seasonal (matching the April cash-flow date of DBRei).

Case Study: Free Lunch in DBRei Apr23?

The effect of the seasonal adjustment gained prominence in 2021. At first glance, German linkers (DBRei) seemed to offer a free lunch. On the screens, the DBRei Apr23 had underperformed massively against ILS and the sovereign peers since May 21 with the break-even rate falling 60bp from the peak to levels highly out of tune with the expected HICP path until April 23.

This mispricing quickly evaporated when factoring in the impact of seasonality on Euro linker valuations. Since May 21, the seasonal adjustment for German linkers had turned very negative as the coupons/notional payment were due in April, which has a very negative seasonal effect as the three-month lag CPI effect makes the typically large HICP decline in January the reference point. For this reason, the quoted real yield of the DBRei was higher than if correctly adjusted for this seasonality.

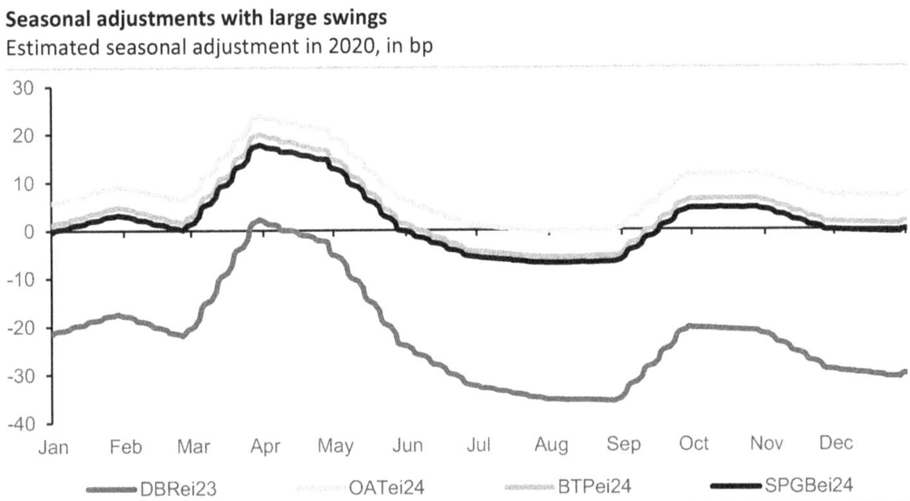

Figure 5.10: 2020 seasonal adjustment.
Source: Bloomberg, Commerzbank Research.

For the DBRei Apr23, we estimated a seasonal adjustment of 55bp; that is, the adjusted real yield of the bond was 55bp lower and the break-even 55bp higher if seasonality/the inflation accrual is correctly being accounted for (see the left-hand chart in Figure 5.11). As the right-hand chart in Figure 5.11 highlights, on a seasonality-adjusted basis the DBRei Apr23 and OATei Jul24 break-evens traded in a synchronized way throughout the period.

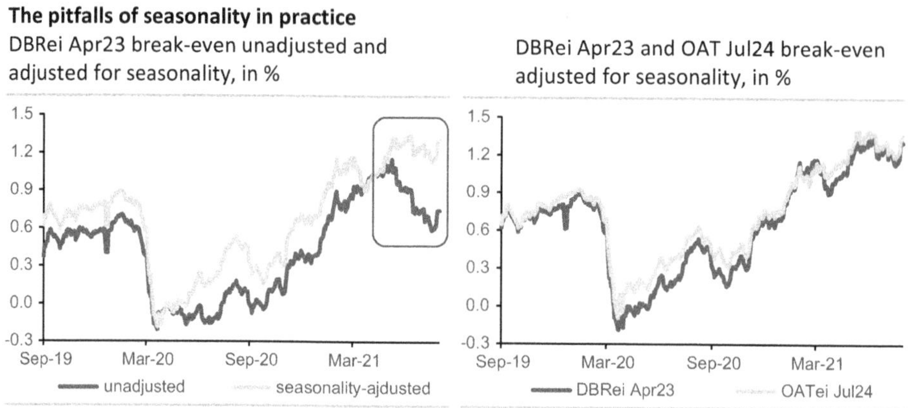

Figure 5.11: Seasonality adjustments.
Source: Eurostat, Bloomberg, Commerzbank Research.

Inflation Curves from ILS

Accounting for seasonality is also important for constructing meaningful inflation curves. For practical purposes, like the valuation of derivatives or the computation of linker ASW-spreads, CPI and forward inflation rates for intermediate months (or days) are typically required.

Incorporating seasonality is therefore crucial in order to obtain correct monthly (and daily) reference index values and inflation curves (see Figure 5.12 and Chapter 3 for a more detailed discussion).

Distortions in the Seasonal Pattern During the Pandemic

The Covid-19 pandemic and the resulting lockdowns led to significant changes in the consumption pattern and distortions in price surveys. The harmonized consumer price index is a so-called Laspeyres index. This means that price changes in year t are weighted by the consumer expenditure structure of year t−1.[4] As this is usually not yet known at the beginning of a year, the expenditure structure of year t-2 is used for practical reasons. In 2021, however, the estimated expenditure structure during the coronavirus pandemic in 2020 formed the basis for the annual HICP reweighting.

4 This distinguishes the Harmonized Index of Consumer Prices for the euro area from many national price indices (including that for Germany). In these, the price development of individual goods is aggregated over several years with constant weights based on consumer spending in a base year. At present, this is generally the year 2015.

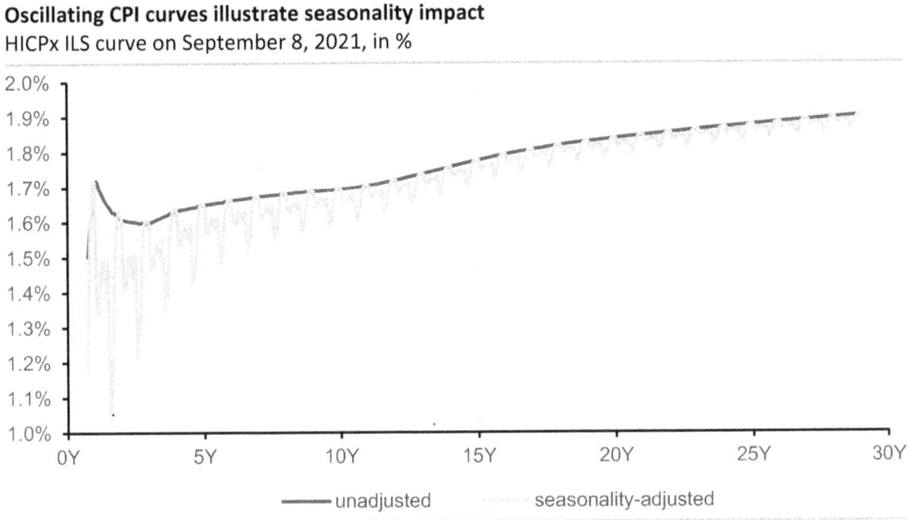

Figure 5.12: Oscillating seasonality impact.
Source: Eurostat, Bloomberg, Commerzbank Research.

During the lockdowns in the pandemic many prices could not be obtained. For example, the Federal Statistical Office of Germany lacked price observations for 86 percent of clothing and footwear and 70 percent for restaurants and accommodation services in April 2020, in which cases prices are extrapolated or estimated. Moreover, the seasonal pattern shifted as summer and winter sales for clothing were pushed back a few weeks in several countries.

In addition to the direct impact on prices, the expenditure structure also changed significantly during the lockdowns with the temporary closure of hotels, restaurants, cinemas, theaters, museums, hair salons and large parts of the retail sector. Spending on package holidays was cut to a third of previous levels, and spending on restaurant and accommodation services to a half. Accordingly, the weights of these goods in the basket fell sharply in 2021. The upshot is that, for example, the usual significant price fluctuations of package holidays will have had a much smaller impact on the monthly change in the overall HICP in 2021, due to their greatly reduced weight.

The combination of unsteady price observations and significant shifts in the basket weights thus lead to distortions not only in the year-on-year HICP inflation rates but also in the month-on-month pattern and thus deformed the typical seasonal pattern, certainly in 2021 and 2022 and possibly in subsequent years.

Seasonality-adjusted HICP changes allow us to put the underlying dynamics into context as we can thereby decompose a given m/m rate into a constant trend and a seasonal factor. Figure 5.13 highlights the magnitude of the changing consumption patterns on 2021 HICP: the seasonality-adjusted m/m change in January 2021 exceeded the increase implied by a constant annual inflation of 2 percent by the largest difference on record and was followed by persistent upside deviations throughout 2021.

Base Effects Explained

Understanding the underlying drivers of CPI dynamics is key for putting deflation or overshooting fears into context. Isolating mechanical from structural developments is not straightforward though, with base effects in particular being mixed up with other concepts.

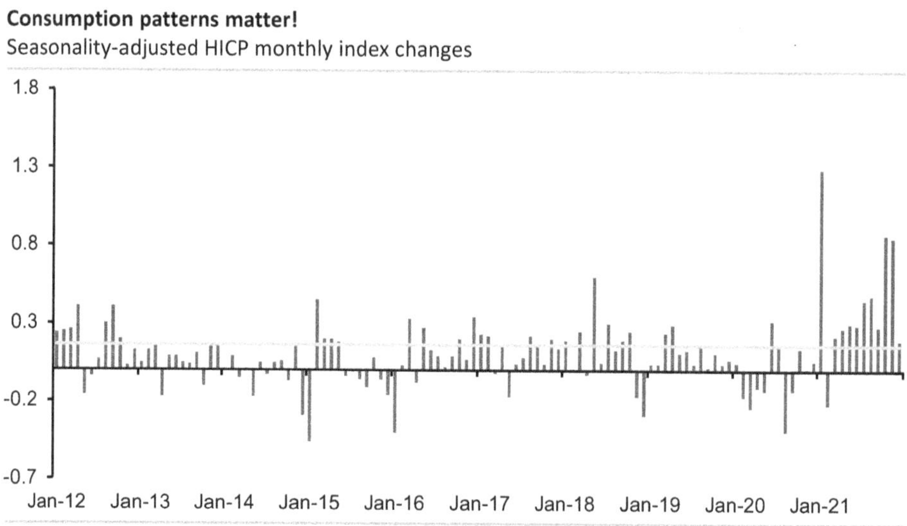

Figure 5.13: Seasonality-adjusted HICPx monthly changes.
Source: ECB, Commerzbank Research.

Why are Base Effects Important?

Energy prices are typically a key driver of short-term swings in headline inflation. Multiple forces are at play though with varying impact on monthly CPI figures. Digging deeper into the underlying components can thus uncover additional value and a better understanding of the risk-profile of CPI releases – and hence the likely central bank response.

Isolating mechanical from structural developments in inflation is not straightforward, with base effects in particular being mixed up with different concepts like seasonality. Furthermore, month-on-month (m/m) and year-on-year (y/y) considerations can also give rise to confusion. We therefore provide a comprehensive overview of base effects and the implications for investors.

Base Effects Capture Past Price Developments

Market participants typically focus on year-on-year inflation rates. These are impacted by both current and past price dynamics of the underlying components. Base effects capture the carry-over of past price dynamics into the current year-on-year rate, that is, how much of the change in the inflation rate is due to price changes in the past twelve months dropping out of the year-on-year comparison.

A few technical observations illustrate the point. The change in the year-on-year rate between any two months can be decomposed into the change in the current month-on-month rate and the month-on-month rate twelve months earlier.

The change in the latter – that is, the month-on-month rate twelve months earlier – captures the base effect, in line with the ECB's definition (ECB 2005). Put differently, base effects capture the contribution of past price dynamics to the current headline rate.

An example: If energy prices have increased sharply twelve months ago (month-on-month), these developments during the base month will now drop out of the year-on-year comparison – and thus mechanically push the current year-on-year rate lower. Other examples are one-off changes in the underlying CPI basket, as is repeatedly the case with the accounting for package holidays in the German CPI or changes in indirect taxes with value-added tax (VAT) cuts the most prominent example, as are administered prices.

Accordingly, base effects and their mechanical impact on annual headline CPIs can be projected twelve months into the future.

Figures 5.14 and 5.15 highlight the crucial contribution of base effects to the headline number in the case of HICP. In March/April 2021, for example, energy base effects explained more than 0.75 percentage points of the increase in the headline rate as the deterioration in energy prices at the height of the pandemic in 2020 dropped out of the year-on-year comparison. Likewise, sharply negative base effects are set to weigh on headline HICP early next year.

Throughout the pandemic, base effects have had a profound influence on the index levels.

What is the Difference Between Base Effects and Seasonality?

Seasonality Captures Current Dynamics

Price indices do not rise smoothly but exhibit substantial swings over the course of the year. The price decline for clothing typically observable in January on the back

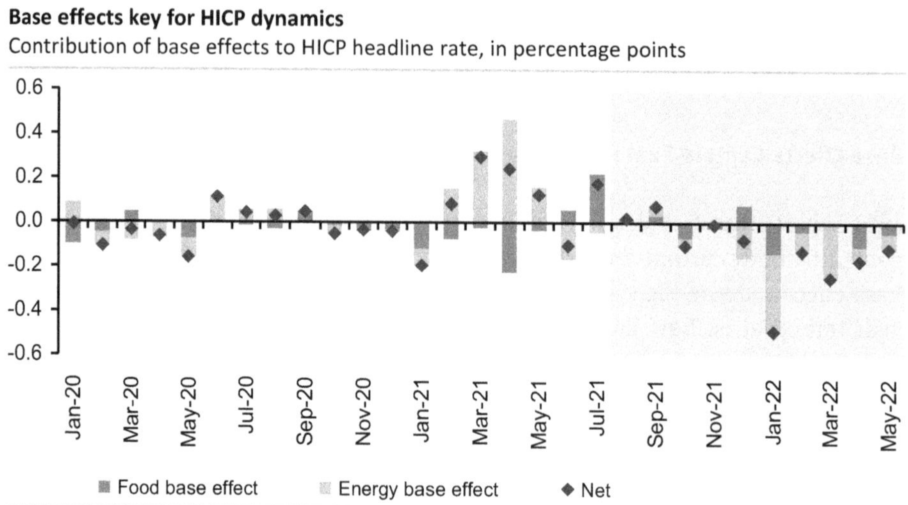

Figure 5.14: Base effects for HICPx.
Source: Eurostat, Bloomberg, Commerzbank Research.

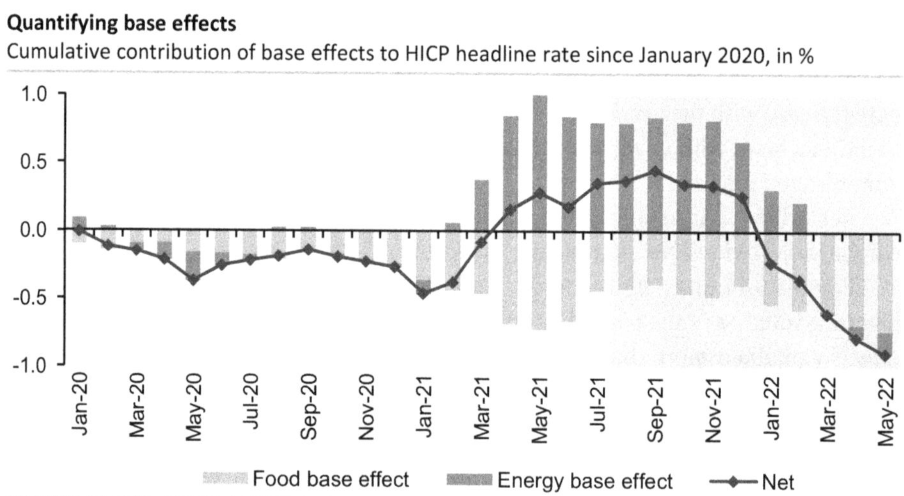

Figure 5.15: Cumulative base effects for HICP.
Source: Eurostat, Bloomberg, Commerzbank Research.

of post-Christmas sales is a prominent example. In a nutshell, seasonality incorporates these re-occurring and predictable deviations from the underlying trend rate.

Seasonality thus captures the price dynamics of the current month, in contrast to base effects, which capture changes in the base month, that is, the past. Furthermore, seasonality is confined to month-on-month rates, as there is by definition no seasonality in year-on-year terms.

Judgment is Crucial

That said, the boundary between base effects and seasonality is not always clear-cut. Seasonal patterns can change over time and thus also affect year-on-year rates. Monthly changes in, say, energy or clothing prices can deviate significantly from what the typical seasonal patterns would suggest. While technically a base effect (as the change in the current m/m rate deviates from the m/m rate twelve months ago), current price dynamics and thus seasonality can be the underlying driver.

Judgment is therefore required to determine whether this represents a structural change – that is, a change in the seasonality pattern – or a one-off event affecting the current month only. The latter interpretation would argue for a base effect in twelve months' time.

This holds true above all for the changes in HICP item weights in 2021, which result from changing consumption patterns during the pandemic. For various items, these adjustments were the largest on record many times over.

Chapter 6
Risk Measures and Risk Premia

Risk and Inflation-Linked Products

Inflation-linked products are subject to a somewhat unique set of risks and risk premia, and once more it's essential to understand what is going on to trade these products. What do we mean by these two terms?

The risk of a product is assumed to be some measure of its price variability. A high-risk product is one whose value varies greatly. A low-risk product has a stable value. Even as we make these statements, a question arises – why are we saying "variability" and not "loss likelihood"? If there were a product that tended to make sharp price gains but not losses, its risk indicated by price variability would nevertheless be high, even though its "risk" in the intuitive, probability-of-bad-things-happening way would seem low. Let's park this thought for the time being though it will return later in the chapter.

If we can say then that price variability is "risk" then we usually use the label "volatility." This has a formal definition – the standard deviation of returns – which itself also makes assumptions, chief among these being that the return distribution is normal. Again, let's park this for later, and proceed with volatility as a risk measure.

Risk premia layer another unwelcome component onto an already tricky subject. The inflation risk premium (IRP) is a consequence of uncertainty. Inflation-linked products trade at a spread to similar nominal counterparts, and this spread is due to both the expected value of genuine inflation, and a risk premium that compensates for the uncertainty surrounding future inflation. Though it is an intuitive concept, it is surprisingly difficult to estimate these two components. Despite considerable effort over the years, academics and market practitioners still struggle to extract information from inflation-linked products about the evolution of the IRP. A number of models use market data like ILBs or ILS as inputs, but the IRP time series that they generate frequently closely resemble these input data series, with little new information. As a consequence, market-based (i.e., product price-based) measures of longer-term inflation fluctuate only via the IRP, while genuine inflation expectations seem stable – with implications for positioning, issuance, risk management and policy decisions.

As we have shown in Chapter 2, it's possible to create a term structure of the yield difference between inflation-linked bonds and their nominal counterparts. Naively, one might expect that this difference is the expected value of future inflation. But that's not all it is. There may be an expected mean value of inflation but there is also uncertainty about what this value will be (i.e., a distribution around this mean). The difference in yield between nominal bonds and ILBs (the inflation

https://doi.org/10.1515/9783110787429-006

compensation or IC) will include an additional offset (the inflation risk premium [IRP]) to compensate for this uncertainty. Finally, it is generally thought that there is another bias to adjust for the lower liquidity of ILBs compared to their nominal equivalents, the so-called liquidity premium (LP).

Thus, the subject of risk needs to be understood in terms of

(1) What is it really all about? In this case, the value of future inflation.
(2) What metric are you using? If it is a simple estimate like the SPF delivers, fine. But if it is a market traded product then . . .
(3) What else is your metric including? What other risks/risk premia are embedded within its value and variation?

To get a good handle on the likely values of future inflation, a good understanding of the above points is essential.

Risk Measures

There is a decent amount of confusion regarding this topic, warranting special diligence when quantifying the risk of inflation-linked bonds. Numerous risk measures tend to be higher for linkers than for nominal bonds. This seems somewhat counterintuitive given that linkers are typically perceived to be less risky than their nominal peers.

Common Risk Measures May Give a Distorted Picture

Duration for linkers can be calculated as for conventional bonds; duration captures the percentage change of a bond price, given a change in real yield-to-maturity. The computation remains the same if computed for a real or a nominal price (keep in mind that the nominal price is simply the real price multiplied by the index ratio).

$$\frac{dP_{real}}{P_{real}} = -Dur \times dr_{real}$$

$$\frac{dP_N}{P_N} = \frac{dP_{real} \times IR}{P_{real} \times IR} = -Dur \times dr_{real}$$

Regarding PVBP (present value per basis point), that is, absolute price changes, we have to specify whether the risk refers to the real or the nominal price, however. As market participants are interested in changes in nominal prices for a 1 basis point change in yields, the nominal PBVP is therefore the appropriate risk measure.

Adjusting the above formulas accordingly yields the following metrics:

$$dP_{real} = -(Dur \times dr_{real}) \times dr_{real} = PVBP_{real} \times dr_{real}$$

$$dP_N = dP_{real} \times IR = PVBP_{real} \times IR \times dr_{real}$$

$$PVBP_N = PVBP_{real} \times IR$$

Hence, the appropriate PVBP for setting up positions in inflation-linked bonds is the real PVBP multiplied by the index ratio (done implicitly in markets where bonds are quoted in nominal terms). These risk measures thus vary with the progression of the index ratio even if everything else remains equal. This also implies that seasoned bonds tend to have a higher PVBP given their typically higher IR.

PVBP for Linkers Higher Than for Nominals, But Real Yields are Less Volatile

Linkers tend to have smaller coupons and lower yields than comparable nominal bonds. Thus, back-end cash-flows contribute a larger share to the present value of the ILB due to the resulting lower discounting rates. Put differently, a change of 1 basis point in the ILB yield has a greater impact on its price, making them appear "riskier" compared to their nominal counterparts. This seems counter-intuitive given that linkers are usually alleged to be less risky than nominal bonds.

However, one has to distinguish between changes in the real yield of the linker and the nominal yield of a conventional bond.

From theory . . .

Both yields are well correlated – recall that real yields are a component of nominal yields. In a nutshell, textbooks state that nominal yields are driven by growth and inflation expectations while real yields are only impacted by the growth component (in accordance with the Fisher equation). At the same time, growth and inflation expectations are typically positively correlated. Hence, real yields and break-evens move in sync, causing nominal yields to rise upon improving growth expectations, and more so than real yields.

Put differently, the underlying mathematics suggest that real yields are on balance less volatile than nominals as they are not affected by variations in expected inflation (i.e., break-evens[1]). Thus, while the price change for a given yield change is higher for ILBs, the magnitude of real yield changes is likely to be smaller than

1 As long as the covariance between real yields (r_y) and break-even inflation (BEI) is not sharply negative, real yields are less volatile than nominal yields (n). Technically, the Fisher equation discussed in Chapter 2 implies that $\sigma_n{}^2 = \sigma_{ry}{}^2 + \sigma_{BEI}{}^2 + 2\ \mathrm{cov}(r_y, \mathrm{BEI})$.

that of nominal yield changes. In other words, linkers are typically less risky than their nominal counterparts.

. . . To Practice

In practice, however, the empirical evidence suggests that these statements don't always apply. The realized basis point volatility of 10y implied euro real versus nominal swap rates serves as a decent proxy for the volatility differential, delivering a consistent picture over longer time horizons irrespective of changing issuance patterns and roll-down of ILBs.

Figure 6.1 highlights that although ILS tend to exhibit a lower realized volatility than nominals, the volatility differential collapses during stress periods. In addition, the implicit nominal yield cap combined with tolerance for inflation overshooting that most central banks tend to implicitly encourage suggests that the bulk of adjustments has to be driven by real rather than nominal yields.

In technical terms, the 2008 crisis and the central bank response gave rise to periods of negative covariance between real yields and break-evens, hence lowering the volatility advantage of inflation-linked products.

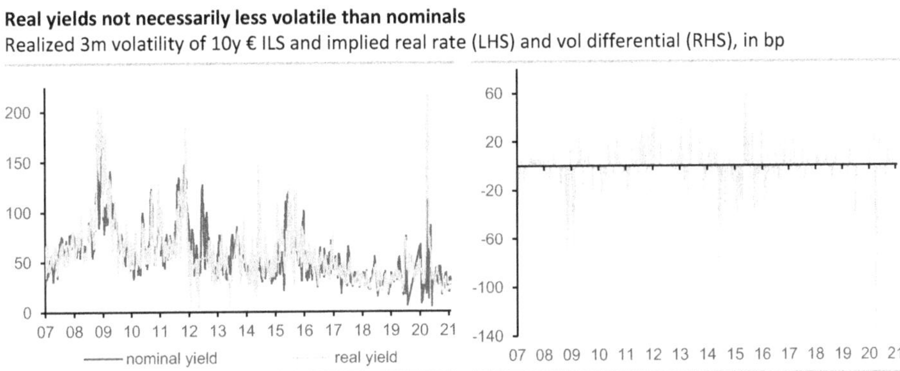

Figure 6.1: Real and implied yields.
Source: Bloomberg, Commerzbank Research.

A key factor is that although the positive correlation between growth and inflation expectations that is stated by the textbooks is typically observable in practice, it does not always hold.

Figure 6.2 highlights that fluid relationship. During the US-driven reflation selloff in Q1-2021, positive US data surprises and improving global macro prospects were accompanied by rising break-evens and real yields, as one would have expected, pushing nominal yields to new cyclical highs. From May 2021 to the end of the year, however, the fading global growth optimism together with data disappointments pushed real yields lower but did not trigger falling inflation expectations. To the

Growth and inflation expectations are not always positively correlated
Commerzbank US Economic Surprise Indicator (activity data) versus 5y5y € ILS in % (lhs) versus implied 5y5y euro real yield (rhs) in %

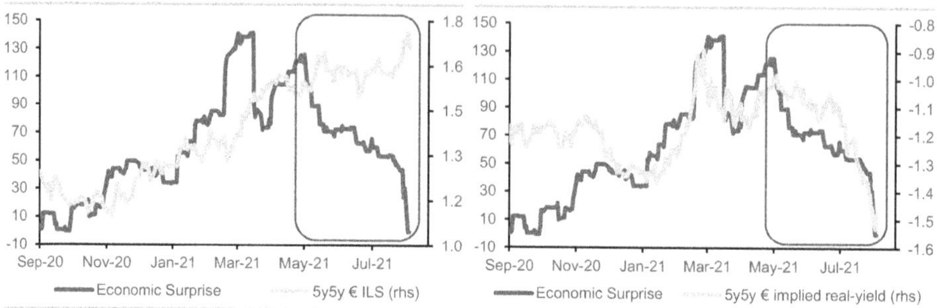

Figure 6.2: Growth vs inflation expectations.
Source: Bloomberg, Commerzbank Research.

contrary, the deterioration in the data flow had been accompanied by new multi-year highs in break-evens (see the left-hand chart in Figure 6.2) while real yields sank in textbook fashion (see the right-hand chart in Figure 6.2).

The Beta Concept

A higher volatility of nominal yields relative to their real counterparts has significant implications for the hedging of ILBs. One way that markets try to capture the extent to which real and nominal yields move in sync, and to hence derive the effective nominal duration of a linker, is via the beta factor.

Technically, "beta" is the regression coefficient of an ordinary least squares (OLS) regression of changes in real yields on changes in nominal yields. A straightforward interpretation is "how much does the real yield change given a 1 basis point nominal yield change"? A very low beta suggests that real yields move only marginally and that the remaining component of nominal yield changes stems from break-evens. Note that in this case adding linkers to a nominal portfolio generates substantial diversification benefits. Conversely, for betas above one, real yields move more than nominal yields, implying that break-evens must move in opposite direction to real yields. For a beta close or equal to one, real yields and nominal yields move in sync. Note also that a plain vanilla break-even trade implicitly assumes a beta of one, as it is precisely the change of the break-even inflation that is targeted. This is also the default assumption for the yield and spread analysis (YAS) function on Bloomberg. Historically, beta tends to be smaller than one, underpinning the claim that linkers are less volatile. Linkers can therefore be deemed less risky than nominals and thus provide diversification benefits.

As before, however, such statements don't apply in all market environments. Betas are not stable over time and depend on the time frame as well as the maturity of the instrument used to derive it (see Figure 6.3). Over the past decade, beta has been virtually fixed at about one for both euro and dollar inflation products amid very marginal fluctuations. Hence, real and nominal yields have been moving closely in sync until summer 2020 when break-evens took off and real yields trended sideways.

This break-down accelerated in summer 2021 with real yields moving faster than nominals and in the opposite direction of inflation break-evens (see Figure 6.3 for implied 5y5y real rates, and the picture looks similar when using ILBs). Unconventional monetary policy measures like the introduction/tapering of asset purchases as well as a more recent shift towards implicit nominal yield caps and inflation overshooting have further increased the beta instability with beta even rising above one. Beta hedging of linkers with nominals thus contains risks and these conceptual limitations should be kept in mind.[2]

Beta hedging is not without pitfalls given instability over time

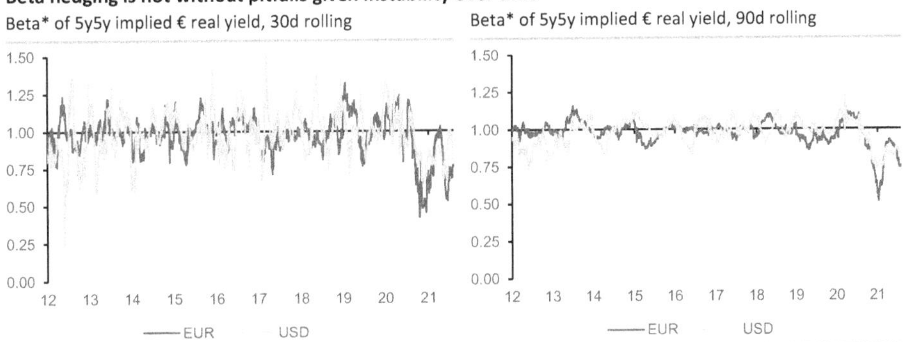

Figure 6.3: Beta hedging.
Source: Eurostat, Bloomberg, Commerzbank Research.

Risk Premia

The (il)liquidity premium

The (il)liquidity and inflation risk premiums can become significant drivers of inflation-linked products. In Chapter 2, we calculated cash break-even rates as a yield spread between a nominal and an indexed-linked bond of similar maturity and credit

2 The technically correct way to quantify the duration of a break-even position (or any portfolio containing inflation-linked and nominal bonds) is by calculating the duration with respect to real yields and the duration with respect to inflation expectations. Note that these are the components of the Fisher equation discussed in Chapter 2. Likewise, a little algebra shows that beta = $cov(r_y, n_y) / vol_{ny}$.

quality. Besides changing inflation expectations, a change in the liquidity premium can also trigger swings in the break-even rates observable on cash markets.

Liquidity Differentials Can Substantially Impact Cash Break-evens

By simply subtracting real and nominal yields, we implicitly assume that nominal and inflation-linked bonds are equally liquid. The market reality is different though, as linkers are typically less liquid than their nominal peers. Investors demand a higher yield for a less liquid instrument and linker yields therefore contain a liquidity premium over their nominal counterparts.

This is compounded by the higher credit exposure of linkers due to the back-loaded nature of cash-flows. Particularly during stress periods investors demand a compensation for the lower liquidity of ILBs, triggering downside pressure on break-evens that is unrelated to inflation expectations (and/or inflation risks). For that reason, BTPei break-evens also tend to underperform their higher-rated ILB peers during stress periods.

The liquidity premium weighs on break-evens in cash bond space, thus resulting in a downward bias for this proxy for the market's underlying inflation expectations. This is particularly relevant for 5–10y German linkers, as (nominal) Bunds are more liquid than their French and Italian peers given CTD-eligibility for the benchmark Bund and Bobl futures. Moreover, the liquidity premium is not stable over time but can fluctuate substantially, typically increasing during periods of market stress. Due to these swings in the liquidity premium, quoted cash break-even rates can thus swing significantly even in the case of unchanged underlying inflation expectations.

A Proxy

We approximate the liquidity premium by subtracting the seasonality-adjusted break-even rate in bond space from the break-even rate of maturity-matched inflation swap (equivalent to the IOTA-spread; for details see Chapter 3). Although the level of this approximation should be taken with a pinch of salt as ILS trade structurally higher than ILBs on the back of supply and demand imbalances, we believe that this approach captures the dynamics of the (il)liquidity premium quite well. It therefore provides valuable information for positioning in linker space.

The liquidity premium can be highly significant, in particular during episodes of market stress, as highlighted in Figure 6.4. It also exhibits substantial swings over time.

The Inflation Risk Premium

The inflation risk premium (IRP) has established itself as a pivotal factor for policy makers and investors; it is, for example, a central factor in the ECB's reaction function

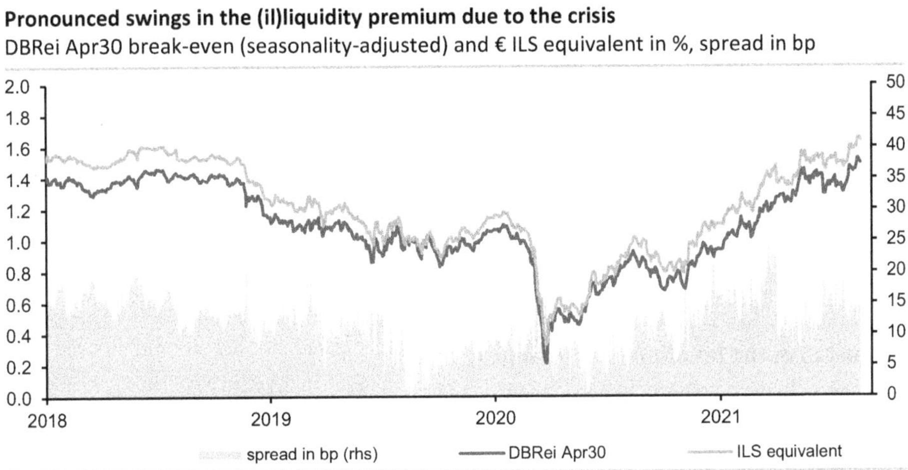

Figure 6.4: Liquidity premium.
Source: Bloomberg, Commerzbank Research.

with executive board members repeatedly ascribing a large part of the fluctuations in longer-term OIS rates and break-evens to swings in the IRP. However, there is no one accepted way of measuring this important though elusive quantity!

As a rule of thumb: the higher the upside risks for inflation, the higher the premium that investors demand for holding conventional bonds. This follows from the fact that the real return of a nominal bond is uncertain ex-ante, while it is known for linkers due to linkage of real coupons and principal to CPIs (see also Chapter 2). Therefore, higher uncertainty regarding inflation – and hence nominal returns – is often taken to imply higher break-even rates.

The global disinflation backdrop and significant deflation fears in early 2015 turned this argument upside down however, particularly as investors are more sensitive to deflationary shocks compared to rising inflation. In essence, "high inflation" typically occurs in a positive economic and macro environment, while deflation tends to occur in periods of simultaneous stress on financial markets and an adverse macroeconomic shock (see Fleckenstein 2013 for more detail).

In turn, the IRP is one of the few risk measures that central bankers are sometimes happy to see increasing, especially after it declined to unprecedented levels and nominal bonds changed from being an "inflation bet" to a "deflation hedge."

As investors are also typically risk averse, quoted inflation caps and floors – which reflect the market price of hedging inflation uncertainty – not only reflect genuine inflation uncertainty, but also include general risk and liquidity premia as well as a premium to hedge deflation tail risks (risk-neutral versus physical probabilities in technical terms). For more detail on extracting information about future inflation from the inflation option market see Chapter 7.

These observations illustrate that a declining inflation risk premium cannot always be equated to declining inflation uncertainty and vice versa. Given the global disinflation backdrop since the Lehman crisis up until recently, it is not necessarily uncertainty regarding inflation itself that drives the IRP, but the balance of inflation being below or above a certain threshold: if deflation fears rise or reflation expectations fall the IRP declines and vice versa (ECB 2017).

Likewise, it is not so much uncertainty regarding a single CPI release but the consistency of consecutive CPI surprises that impact the IRP.

Estimates of the Inflation Risk Premium

Clearly it would be useful to have an unbiased (risk-neutral) estimate of the expected future inflation. And, for sovereign debt management purposes, issuers would be interested in the size of the IRP as they effectively pay this premium when issuing nominal bonds. When issuing ILBs, a positive risk premium would lead to lower costs for the issuer. In addition, the size and sign of the IRP offer valuable information for policy makers to help interpret market signals about the inflation process.

Previous Calculation Methods and Results

There is a plethora of methods used to calculate the IRP, mostly focused on US inflation. The inputs to the different models include

- the break-even inflation rate
- survey-based expectations
- ILB yields
- nominal bond yields
- realized inflation
- other macro data

Most use ILBs as a key input, but more recently ILS have also been utilized. The models themselves are also tremendously varied. It is common to use the difference between survey results and market-based measures as a starting point, and also common to use affine[3] term structure models that assume that the difference between real and risk neutral yield curves is due to the presence of risk premia. The majority of published work acknowledges that however a risk premium is extracted, it will be a combination of inflation risk premium and liquidity premium. There is a limited supply of inflation-linked government debt, and this can strongly affect

3 An affine term structure model implies that the log of the zero coupon bond prices are linear functions of the spot rate.

liquidity and thus prices and yields. The inflation risk premium and the liquidity premium are extremely difficult to separate, and attempts to do so tend to rely on various liquidity proxies. One answer to this issue is to substitute ILS for ILB, as they may be less affected by any liquidity premium or credit aspects, as discussed above, and one would expect to see more work in this area as more ILS data becomes available (see Burban 2021 for a recent note on the subject).

To summarize the current set of estimates, derived by the different approaches discussed above, see Figure 6.5. The boxes each represent one model, and their top and bottom levels are the maximum and minimum value of the IRP that they derive. The left and right edges of each box are the start and end of the data set used over which the IRP is calculated.

With this visualization of the data it is obvious that the great majority of models and methods have concentrated on a single decade, and that, overall, they do not agree on values for the IRP! It would be pleasing to be able to plot time series for each of these models, but we were not able to find available data; the maximum and minimum values were easier to discover. Inflation risk premia calculations and results also suffer from the problem that risk premia tend to be correlated. It is not uncommon to create a graph using one method that closely resembles the result from an apparently different method – but a closer look at the input data will often reveal commonalities that were there from the start.

Keeping it Simple

To illustrate the merits of keeping things simple and not over-thinking (or over-calculating), we can take a look at a state-of-the-art model used by the ECB mentioned in a 2021 presentation[4] by Isabel Schnabel, a member of the ECB executive board. This approach uses an affine term structure model and compensations for lagged data to create a time series for the 10y EUR inflation risk premium. It appears to only take the ILS rates as inputs. We contrast it with a simple technique, where we just take the difference of the liquid 5y5y ILS rate and the EU Survey of Professional Forecasters' (SPF) estimates of what inflation will be in 5 years' time. It is clear that various different models and methods have pointed to the difference between survey-based inflation forecasts and market-derived implied future inflation values being a key input to the inflation risk premium. It is also apparent that separating the "pure" inflation risk premium from bond liquidity premia is difficult, so it makes sense to use the ILS data rather than ILB where possible. Below we graph the SPF and ILS data in Figure 6.6 on the left, and their difference together with the ECB calculation of the IRP, in Figure 6.6 on the right.

4 Isabel Schnabel, member of the ECB executive board Petersberger Sommerdialog, presentation given July 3, 2021.

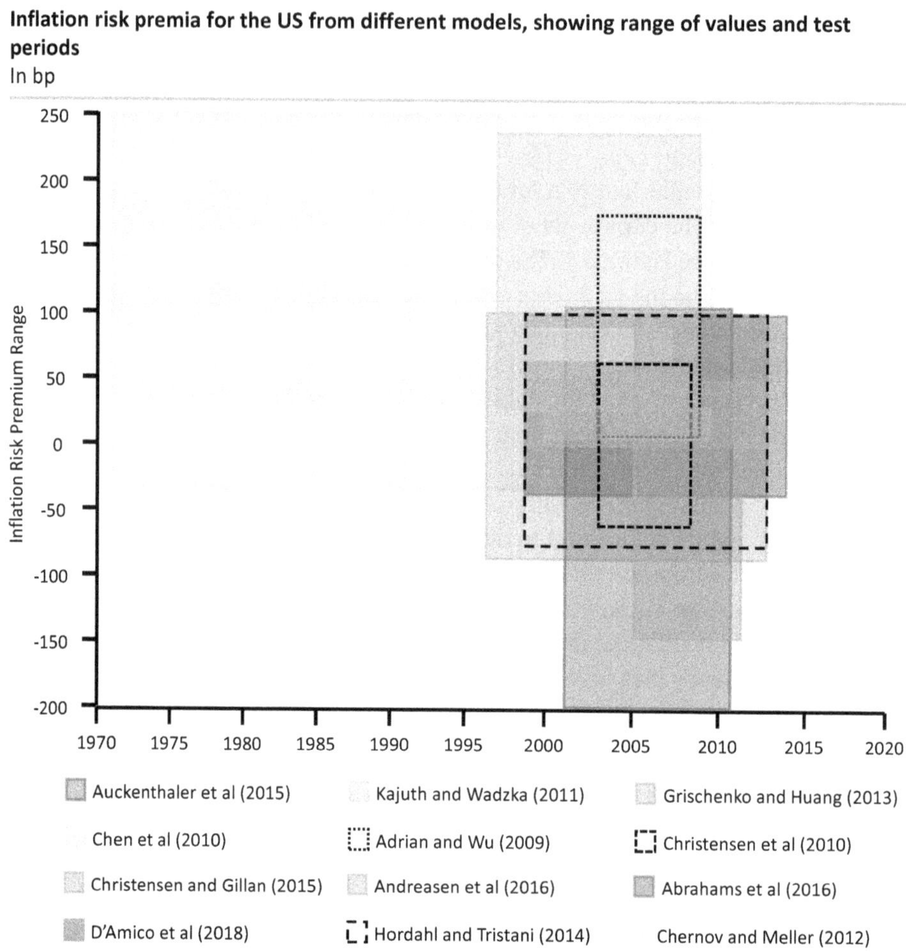

Figure 6.5: Schematic of previous inflation risk premia published results.
Source: Commerzbank Research, see Appendix for other references.

The simple difference model appears to contain all the information in the more complex affine model used by the ECB – note also that both measures are on the same y-axis, that is, they agree on the basis point level as well as the evolution. It seems that the modeling process may just be a recasting of the input data.

We can repeat the above exercise with US data. In Kim et al. (2019) from the FEDS Notes series of papers, the authors use an affine term structure model to decompose the US Treasury Inflation Protected Security (TIPS) Inflation Compensation (calculated as a break-even inflation spread between nominal and inflation protected US government debt) into four components – expected interest rates, expected inflation, inflation risk premium and TIPS liquidity premium. If we take the

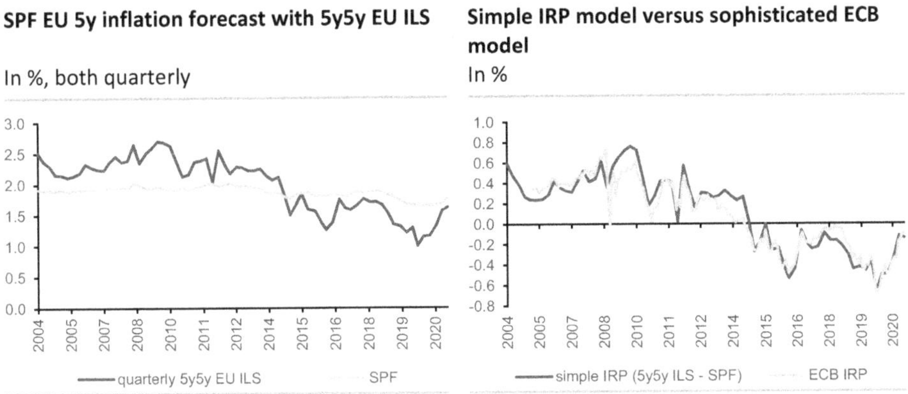

Figure 6.6: Simple and complex EU IRP results.
Source: EU SPF, Bloomberg, ECB, Commerzbank Research.

difference between the US 5y inflation swap and the US Survey of Professional Forecasters' data, then we can assign that to a simple IRP, exactly as above, and then graph this difference together in Figure 6.7 with the TIPS model. Note that the TIPS model gives separate series for pure IRP and liquidity premium, but we recombine them for this comparison.

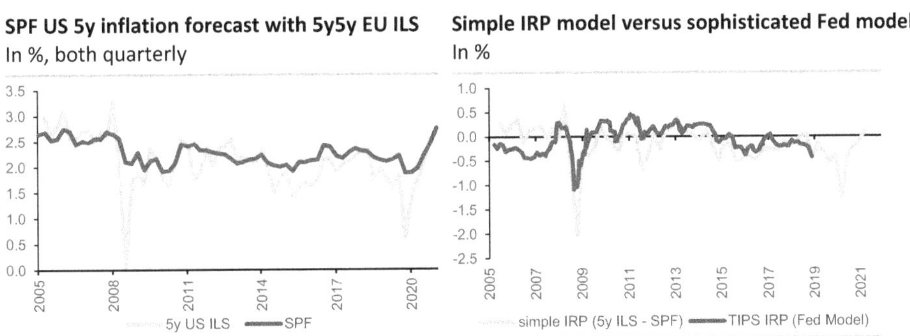

Figure 6.7: Simple and complex US IRP results.
Source: US SPF, Bloomberg, FED, Commerzbank Research.

However, it turns out that a close degree of correspondence is not unique to the simple difference model. It's easy to say, looking at the right-hand graph in Figure 6.7, that all the dynamics of the more complex model are already present in the simple 5y ILS series, and that taking away the fairly constant SPF series only adjusts the overall level.

In Figures 6.8 and 6.9, for the euro area and the USA, we chart the simple IRP and the more sophisticated affine model derived version, first with the 10y inflation swap for the relevant market, and then with the option derived deflation probability from the option market (this data is only available more recently). The only significant difference in the various series is the overall level – note that some series use a secondary axis. But as to information content, it is difficult to see that anything is added apart from a general scale or level factor.

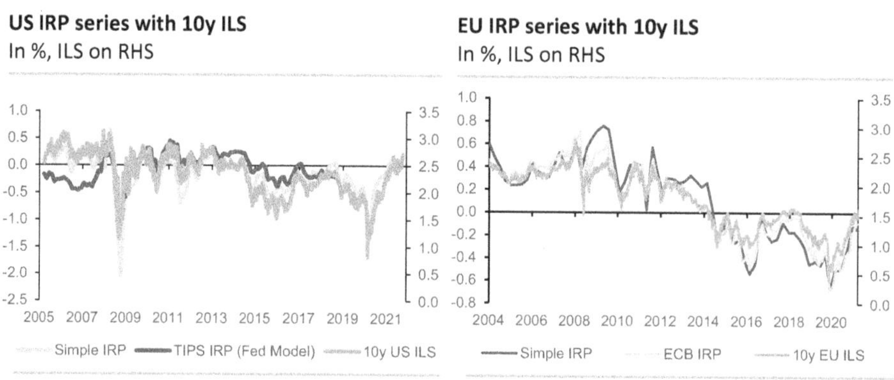

Figure 6.8: IRP results with 10y ILS.
Source: US SPF, EU SPF, Bloomberg, ECB, FED, Commerzbank Research.

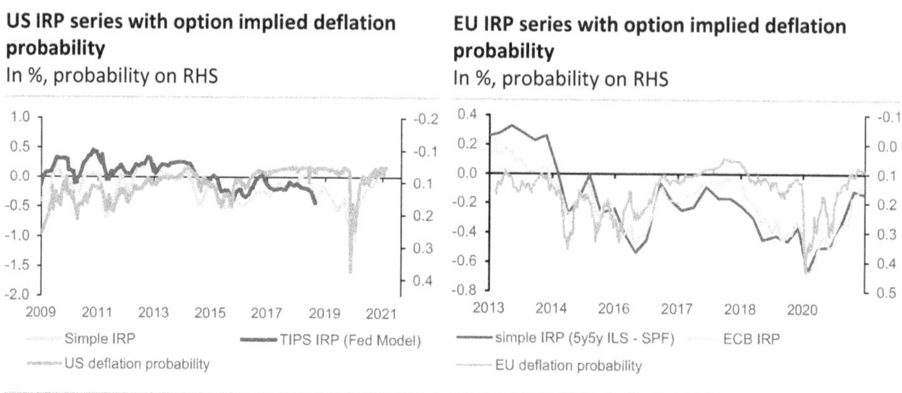

Figure 6.9: IRP results with option implied deflation probability.
Source: US SPF, EU SPF, Bloomberg, ECB, FED, Commerzbank Research.

The option implied deflation probabilities are derived as per the method used in Chapter 7 of this book, where we use option derived means and standard deviations from the Minneapolis Fed database for the US data, and assume a normal distribution. For the EU graph, we used the internal Commerzbank SABR model, which has inflation caps and floors as inputs, though, as we will show in Chapter 7, the distribution is close to a normal also.

It would seem that much effort can be expended in different complex and sophisticated ways to arrive at the same conclusions. Results from affine models, detailed analysis of data lags, and option implied probabilities all seem to only differ by a scaling factor. Surely what matters is the sign of the risk, that is, deflation or overshooting. Being able to detect and understand regime changes may perhaps more easily be done with indirect measures like correlation, than the application of detailed analysis that, like the worm Ouroboros, can sometimes end up eating its own tail . . .

What can we conclude? First, that given the focus that markets have on inflation forecasts at the moment, one always needs to keep in mind that inflation expectations derived from market prices do not only reflect genuine expectations regarding future inflation but also an inflation risk premium – and that it is precisely this risk premium that typically determines the dynamic of market-based expectations.

Second, that it is difficult or perhaps impossible to extract more information from the market about future inflation risks than simple approaches provide. Possibly looking at correlations can add information regarding the perceived connectivity of risks and the market view on the best hedge for the future. But for those who struggle to find a reliable way to forecast future inflation – you are not alone, it is one of the most intractable quantities out there, though indeed it is one of the most important.

Third, if the models are right and market-based measures of longer-dated inflation primarily fluctuate via the IRP, the market does not appear to add further information about genuine inflation expectations. Yet, even in that case it would be wrong to neglect the implied levels of inflation embedded in market prices, as they contain other important information about risk premia and market positioning and adjust at much higher frequency to new information than analyst/survey-based forecasts. Also, analyst/survey-based forecasts typically deliver point estimates and thus only part of the whole picture, while inflation markets incorporate the entire distribution. (For an in-depth discussion on the pros and cons of using option-based inflation expectations see Chapter 7.)

Chapter 7
Inflation Options

Capturing the market's view on the range of inflation outcomes is easier said than done. Inflation options have become a popular tool to assess overshooting risks as they capture changes across the entire probability distributions of future euro and US dollar inflation. We dissect the underlying maths, add qualitative factors and show that not all tails are alike. While inflation options provide a robust picture of deflation sentiment, implied expectations on overshooting should not be taken at face value in view of model and liquidity limitations. We assess alternative measures and the implications for investors, issuers and policy makers.

Inflation and Inflation Risks – Why are They Relevant?

Inflation has rarely held the market's attention so closely as it does today. We seem to stand on the cusp of a regime change, from the lowflation of the past decade to an unknown higher range. Though there is talk of a "return to normal," lowflation coupled with unprecedented liquidity injections by central banks has in fact become the "new normal" and markets have become accustomed to life support. Should central banks react according to their mandates, a new, higher inflation regime would hit institutions who have been relying on low cost credit and could cause many of the so-called "zombie" companies to go under – and also challenge the sustainability of ever-rising public debt stocks. Savers, who are facing an erosion of the purchasing power of their savings, would rejoice longer-term when rates normalize and retail banking would have a chance to return to a sustainable "borrow and lend" model.

The likely level of this higher inflation regime and inflation expectations are thus critically important, and widely discussed (ECB 2021a). If the spike in inflation does not trigger higher inflation expectations and second-round effects, policy makers and other economic agents can afford to look through it. Things will look very differently if rising inflation feeds through to longer-dated expectations, changing the underlying inflation dynamics.

In view of the 2 percent inflation targets by most major central banks, it will make a huge difference if underlying inflation settles again at levels closer to, say, 1 percent or 3 percent. And at times when inflation views diverge, so-called linear indications from inflation-linked bonds or swaps only tell half the story if the expected value is, say, at 2 percent while most people think the actual outcome is either below 1 percent or above 3 percent.

https://doi.org/10.1515/9783110787429-007

So, indications of future levels are eagerly sought, and one popular method of obtaining probabilities of a rise to various levels has been the inflation options market. By using methods developed for liquidly traded option markets like equities or interest rates, it becomes possible to derive implied probabilities of inflation changes in the future from the prices of inflation options.

We assess the value and robustness of these indications derived from inflation options, and show that while some parameters are stable and statistically valid, this is not the case for all.

Inflation Options

In inflation markets, the curve that is actively traded and updated is the zero-coupon inflation curve. The "zero-coupon" part refers to the fact that cash-flows occur only on the maturity date and are thus entirely a function of the HICPx level at this maturity date. So, we can get a good handle on the market's opinion of the forward path of inflation. We can even, by looking at the value of the deflation floor, derive a likelihood for deflation. But to derive probabilities for any other inflation scenario, we need option products.

Fortunately, these exist. We discuss the data availability in more detail below, but over the last decade or so, caps and floors that depend on the CPI indices of different countries have evolved. The deepest and most liquid market is probably the EUR market, which uses the HICPx (Harmonised Index of Consumer Prices ex tobacco) as its underlying index. Swaps are traded on the zero-coupon curve derived from this index, and caps and floors are also somewhat liquid and active. In general, these come in two varieties: YoY (year-on-year), which look at the change in the index from one point in the future to a point a year further on, and zero coupon (ZC), which look at the change in inflation from now until the maturity date.

Commerzbank's In-house SABR Model

To extract the implied probability distribution from quoted prices for HICPx caps and floors, a model is required.

Commerzbank (the authors are all working at Commerzbank at the time of writing, and are grateful to be able to present these results) is fortunate in having a sophisticated set of modeling tools for option valuation, which also yield information about implied probabilities for the future. The stochastic alpha, beta, rho (SABR) model (Hagan et al. 2002) is a very useful and flexible model with the flexibility to accommodate skewness and fat tails. It is defined by a linked set of equations, as below:

$$\begin{aligned} dX_t &= \sigma(X_t + d)^{\beta} dW_t \\ d\sigma_t &= \alpha\sigma_t dZ_t \\ dW_t dZ_t &= \rho dt \end{aligned} \tag{1}$$

Here X_t is the variable being modeled, W and Z are random processes, σ is the measure of volatility, α is the volatility of volatility (vol-vol), β is a tail parameter, and r is the correlation between the level of the modeled variable and its volatility. d is a displacement variable that shifts the whole distribution.

Although the interaction among them is complex, each parameter has a clear link to the property it measures. β controls tail width; a normal distribution has a β of zero and a lognormal has a β of 1. α accounts for varying volatility levels, and ρ indicates the degree of parameter correlation that can drive some unexpectedly large market moves.

The model can be used to calculate premia for caps, floors or swaptions in the inflation market. The modeled variable X_t can be the index ratio for zero-coupon options (ratio of inflation at maturity to inflation today) or the period-on-period ratio (ratio of inflation at one future date to inflation at another future date) that are useful for zero-coupon or YoY inflation options respectively.

The inputs to the model are the premia for a set of cap or floor options, which can be zero coupon or YoY, and also the zero-coupon inflation swap curve. The outputs are flexible, and can include option premia for any reasonable strike, fitted parameter values and the probability distribution function (pdf). The pdfs produced by SABR are highly useful in that they can express not only mean and standard deviation, but also the level of skewness and kurtosis implied by the input option prices. Skewness is a measure of the asymmetry of a distribution – distributions with positive skewness have more weight to the higher values, while distributions with negative skewness have more weight to the lower. Kurtosis measures the “fatness” of the tails – its most common definition sets the kurtosis of a normal distribution to be zero, positive values indicate fatter tails than a normal, with negative values indicating thinner or more truncated tails than a normal.

In other words, we can benchmark the distribution extracted from inflation options to other probability distributions (e.g., a simple normal distribution) and thus assess the reliability of option-implied inflation expectations – that is, if the resulting distribution captures actual market dynamics or is primarily a fitting/modeling exercise. Particularly in the context of overshooting (or deflation) concerns, the higher moments of the distribution and their robustness are central.

Such checks are also important as they address the fact that market-based measures of inflation expectations are subject to risk and liquidity premia and hence do not only reflect genuine inflation expectations.

The Minneapolis Fed Data Set

The Federal Reserve Bank of Minneapolis generously makes available an extensive set of time series about US inflation probabilities. For each day since June 2009, it provides a value for the following parameters for the inflation pdf:

- Mean
- Standard deviation
- Skew
- Kurtosis
- 10 percent probability move
- 50 percent probability move (= median)
- 90 percent probability move
- Probability of inflation going to –1 percent or below (large decrease)
- Probability of inflation going to +3 percent or above (large increase)

This data set is available for tenors of 1, 2 and 5 years, though 5 is the longest and best data set, and is the one we focus on here.

While this is a rich and interesting data set, sadly, it does not pin down the distribution! One can imagine that a double-peaked distribution could mimic the parameters of a single peak, or that a degree of "lumpiness" could distort the values. It is however possible to plot the pdf on their website for any selected day and maturity, which is useful.

How have they gone about creating the pdfs that they use to generate the above moments of the distribution? They base their method on the method in Kitsul and Wright (2013), which itself is based on a 1979 paper (Breeden and Litzenberger 1978). The method uses daily quotes on zero-coupon inflation caps at strike prices of 1 percent, 2 percent, 3 percent, 4 percent, 5 percent and 6 percent, and on zero-coupon inflation floors at strike prices of –2 percent, –1 percent, 0 percent, 1 percent, 2 percent and 3 percent. In Kitsul 2013, the authors use these quotes to form implied pdfs for inflation, but without assuming normality. Instead, they initially assume that inflation will only have integer values, which is not as bad as it sounds, if one simply assumes that one will use these points to create a curve. Then, consider a butterfly portfolio that involves buying caps with strikes of k – 1 percent and k + 1 percent while shorting two caps with a strike of k percent. This portfolio is a pure Arrow-Debreu security with a payoff of $1 if inflation is k percent and zero otherwise, for any integer k.

A risk-neutral investor will pay

$$e^{-r_n n} p_{k,n}$$

for this security, where r_n denotes the continuously compounded interest rate for n years and pk,n is the probability that inflation reaches a level of k after n years. They discount by the nominal government term structure. This mechanically yields risk-neutral probabilities of inflation being −2 percent, −1 percent, 0 percent, . . . 5 percent.

For the tails of the pdf, if an investor buys an inflation cap at 5 percent and shorts one at 6 percent, then this investor receives $1 if inflation is 6 percent or more and 0 percent otherwise. This gives the probability of inflation being 6 percent or higher.

The same process works in the left tail as well, for example yielding the probability of inflation being −2 percent or lower. Thus, they create pdfs over different maturities. For this process they use only zero coupon, not YoY, as mathematically the latter is trickier, but it is a pity as the YoY data is generally more liquidly traded.

It seems likely that the Minneapolis Fed study used a similar method, possibly with different granularity for the option strikes dependent upon what data was available.

It is worth noting that the Minneapolis Fed is not the only Central Bank to extract inflation pdfs from inflation option prices, though as far as we are aware it is the only one to make such a generous data set available. One of the others is the Bank of England (BoE 2012), which uses an approach more similar to that of Commerzbank. They use the same initial method by Breeden (1978) to link option prices with an implied pdf, but they interpolate the option prices to give a denser initial data set, which assists with the fitting process, though it does not in itself add information. Finally, they allow the volatility smile (the graph of implied volatility levels versus moneyness) to have flexible properties modeled with the same SABR technique as that used by Commerzbank.

Empirical Observations and Data Limitations

It is clear from the methods outlined above that the essential element for deriving the market-implied future probability distribution of inflation is a set of inflation option premia at different strikes. It is enlightening to go to the raw data and see what goes into the various elegant calculations! To understand what is available, we looked at the EUR inflation option market, which is the most liquid and frequently traded. There are also inflation option prices available for the US, and some individual European countries like the UK, but all of these are likely to have lower liquidity and data availability. We used Bloomberg as our data source, which is generally held to contain all the liquidly traded inflation option products in the euro area.

Underlying Data

Initially, there seems to be a good coverage of strikes, if one searches by listed tickers. There appear to be inflation cap premia with strikes ranging from −1 percent to

+6 percent, in 0.25 percent steps. These would pay out when inflation rises above the specified strike. Inflation floor premia vary similarly from −3 percent to +6 percent. They are available for multiple tenors up to 30 years. So, at a cursory glance one might think that there was a rich data set available. It is worth noting that the ticker names for the various strikes follow no known pattern – the section of the name that indicates the strike goes "A, 3, L" for cap premia of strikes "2.5 percent, 3.0 percent, 3.25 percent." Having gone to the trouble of discovering the ticker names of inflation caps and floors for all the above strikes, it is then possible to look at the data coverage and quality.

Between 6 percent and −1 percent, for the caps, there are 24 tickers (not all steps of 0.25 percent exist). But 24 points is enough to plot a nice smooth curve. However, when one investigates the data feeds, sadly only 8 of these contain data. It is a similar story for the floors, again with only 8 populated strikes. So every pdf extracted, no matter how sophisticated the method used, has come from only 16 points, or 8 if only cap or floor data is used.

Data Limitations

At this stage it is worth a quick look at how easy it is to extract parameters like mean and standard deviation, skew and kurtosis, from distributions, and see what the effect of a small number of data points might be.

As an example, we take the Weibull distribution, a useful analytical form that has parameters that may be adjusted to yield distributions with varying tail thickness, asymmetry, etc. The expression for the distribution is

$$f(x) = \begin{cases} \frac{k}{\lambda}\left(\frac{x}{\lambda}\right)^{k-1} e^{-\left(\frac{x}{\lambda}\right)^k}, & x \geq 0 \\ 0, & x < 0 \end{cases}$$

where k is the shape parameter and λ the scale parameter of the distribution. For our own simple test, we can set scale parameter $\lambda = 1$ to simplify the various expressions, thus although it is mentioned here for completeness, it will not appear again. For this simplified case, you can see in Figure 7.1 what the distribution looks like for $k = 1.5$ and $k = 2.0$.

It is a very popular distributional form used in many applications – engineering, insurance, extreme value theory, weather forecasting and hydrology are just a few examples.[1] Interestingly, it was used by one of the authors to help describe the density variation at the edge of heavy atomic nuclei, in her PhD thesis (James 1994). One

1 https://en.wikipedia.org/wiki/Weibull_distribution is a good general reference for the properties and uses of the Weibull distribution.

Weibull distribution

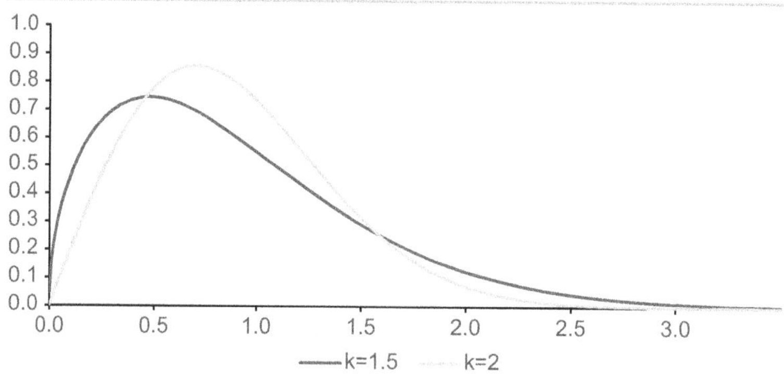

Figure 7.1: Weibull distribution.
Source: Commerzbank Research.

of its many useful features is that it has analytical forms for the values and standard errors of most moments, as we show below.

$$\text{mean } \mu = \Gamma\left(1+\frac{1}{k}\right)$$

$$\text{Standard deviation } \sigma = \left[\Gamma\left(1+\frac{2}{k}\right) - \Gamma\left(1+\frac{1}{k}\right)^2\right]^{1/2}$$

$$\text{skewness } \gamma_1 = \frac{\Gamma\left(1+\frac{3}{k}\right) - 3\mu\sigma^2 - \mu^3}{\sigma^3}$$

$$\text{Kurstosis } \gamma_2 = \frac{\Gamma\left(1+\frac{4}{k}\right) - 4\gamma_1\sigma^3\mu - 6\mu^2\sigma^2 - \mu^4}{\sigma^4}$$

$$\text{standard error for skewness } \sigma(\gamma_1) = \left[\frac{6N(N-1)}{(N-1)(N+1)(N+3)}\right]^{1/2}$$

$$\text{Standard error for kurtosis } \sigma(\gamma_2) = \left[\frac{4(N^2-1)\sigma(\gamma_1)}{(N-3)(N+5)}\right]^{1/2}$$

N is the number of points in the data set. Note that the standard errors assume that there is a numerical data set for the distribution whereas the moments are analytical.

It can easily be seen that the standard errors depend strongly on the number of points in the fit. To check how many points are needed for a reliable estimate of mean, standard deviation, skewness and kurtosis, we generated numerical data for the distributions and the moments, with varying numbers of points, for k = 1.5 and k = 2, and then tabulated the results in Table 7.1.

Table 7.1: Numerical and analytical moments for k = 1.5 and k = 2 Weibull distribution. Numerical results for varying number of data points N.

K=1.5	Mean	Standard Deviation	Skewness	SD(Skewness)	Kurtosis	SD(Kurtosis)
N=12	0.895	0.566	1.633	0.406	2.795	1.518
N=60	0.903	0.609	1.107	0.095	1.466	0.370
N=120	0.903	0.612	1.081	0.049	1.407	0.192
N=600	0.903	0.613	1.071	0.010	1.388	0.040
Analytic	0.903	0.613	1.072		1.390	
K=2.0	**Mean**	**Standard Deviation**	**Skewness**	**SD(Skewness)**	**Kurtosis**	**SD(Kurtosis)**
N=12	0.886	0.427	1.138	0.406	0.864	1.518
N=60	0.886	0.462	0.648	0.095	0.262	0.370
N=120	0.886	0.463	0.635	0.049	0.249	0.192
N=600	0.886	0.463	0.631	0.010	0.245	0.040
Analytic	0.886	0.463	0.631		0.245	

Source: Commerzbank Research.

To understand the tables, first look at the analytic results on the bottom row of each table. These are precise values for the moments calculated with the expressions given above. The numerical results are derived from data sets of the moments generated with the number of points N in the table. Thus, for N = 12, we are attempting to calculate the mean, sd, skewness and kurtosis using only 12 points, and so on.

Looking one line up from the analytic results, that is, N = 600, it can be seen that the numerical results deliver excellent agreement with the analytical – the largest difference is in the kurtosis for k = 1.5 (1.388), which differs only slightly in the final figure from the analytic result (1.390). The standard errors derived using the expressions above for the case of N = 600 are very small.

However, as N gets smaller, the differences and standard errors become very significant. When N = 12, the standard error for skewness is almost as large the skewness value itself, and for the kurtosis in this case, the standard error for the kurtosis is actually larger than the kurtosis value. The numerical results are similarly poor.

In all cases, the results for the mean and standard deviations are close to the true values, indicating that these first two moments are fairly robust to small numbers of points in the fit. When we know that there are at most 8 points in each of the cap and floor data sets, it is clear that the first two moments are likely to be the only reliable ones.

Output from Minneapolis Fed Data Set

Now that it is clear that sparse data sets can have severe limitations, let us take a look at the Minneapolis data set in detail. To gain an initial impression of the data, we can look at a single day's pdf. Figure 7.2 shows the pdf from June 9, 2021, for CPI in five years' time – while the actual pdf data is unavailable for download, we have carefully reproduced this day's pdf in graphic form.

Probability density function for inflation
Data for June 9, 2021, US CPI

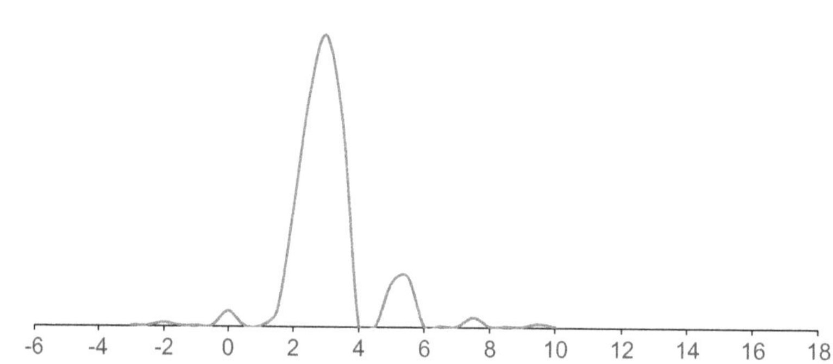

Figure 7.2: Minneapolis Fed pdf.
Source: Minneapolis Fed.

It is immediately clear that the method they are using to extract information from the market has some problems. This pdf has three major peaks and two minor ones in the tails. No-one would suggest that the actual market-implied distribution has these features – on the contrary, it is exactly what one would expect to see from this highly stratified type of method, which, while appealing in its simplicity, needs a densely populated data set to produce realistic results.

Now we take a look at the time series of the moments of the pdf over time, downloaded from the Minneapolis Fed website. The following graphs show mean and standard deviation on the left, with skewness and kurtosis on the right.

While the mean and standard deviation look entirely reasonable, with very realistic values and fairly smooth variation, the same cannot be said for the skewness and kurtosis. The right-hand graph of Figure 7.3 has kurtosis on the left hand (primary) axis, and skewness on the right hand (secondary) axis. Particularly in recent times, both moments show every sign of being heavily affected by fitting problems, with kurtosis varying wildly – for example, on March 10, 2021 it had a value of about 5, but the next data point on March 17, 2021 was more than 28. This is entirely consistent with our earlier investigation of the standard errors for these two moments, which showed that they grow unmanageably large for sparse data sets.

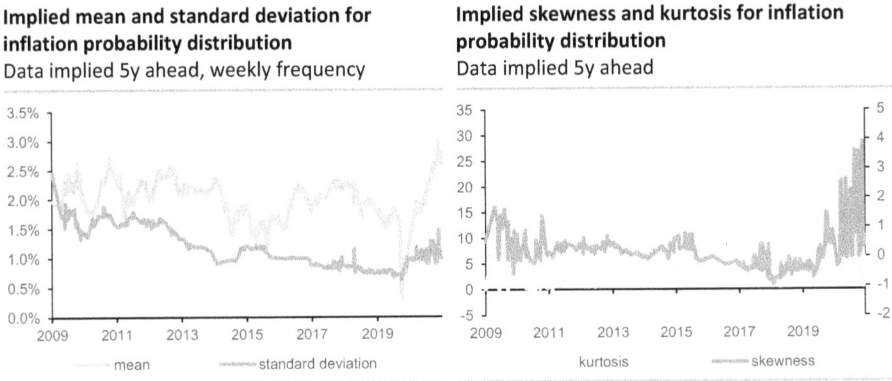

Figure 7.3: Option-implied moments for inflation pdf.
Source: Commerzbank Research.

Output from Commerzbank's SABR Model

The in-house SABR model can be used to sequentially create pdfs on days in history, and the parameters extracted. First, let's take a look at the pdfs which can be derived from single day's data. We have selected two different sources – HICPx inflation index and option data for the EUR market (right-hand graph of Figure 7.4), and interest rates for the EUR market (left-hand graph of Figure 7.4). We have chosen to show the interest rate graph because it is a good demonstration of the flexibility of the model, and because there is a deep and liquid market in options on Euribor, guaranteeing a well populated initial data set.

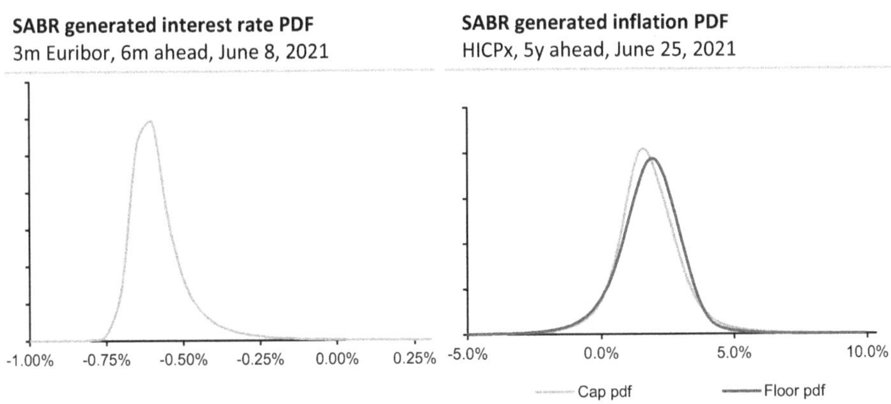

Figure 7.4: SABR generated pdfs.
Source: Commerzbank Research.

It is clear from the interest rate pdf above that the SABR model is very capable of producing distributions that are skewed, and with tails that vary from thin to fat. The inflation pdfs generated at a similar time are symmetrical – caps and floors are separately fitted as each set is likely to be more relevant to different tails of the distribution. However, we can be confident that if there were, on this date, any measurable degree of skewness or kurtosis in the underlying data, it would be well represented in the resulting pdf.

Having established in interest rate data that the SABR model, given sufficient density of input data, can produce realistic pdfs, we can take a look at the parameters of this model through time.

Initially, although we do not plot them here, we find that both β (the tail parameter) and d (the overall displacement) are very close to zero. We might expect d to be close to zero as it is there to allow negative peak values, but the fact that β is zero indicates that, overall, the tails of the distribution are similar to those of a normal distribution. We also find that the σ parameter of the pdfs derived from both cap and floor data are stable and reasonable after mid-2014, but that until mid-2018 there are not sufficient OTM cap and floor options to give stable results for ρ or α. After this date, however, we do have stable results for these two parameters.

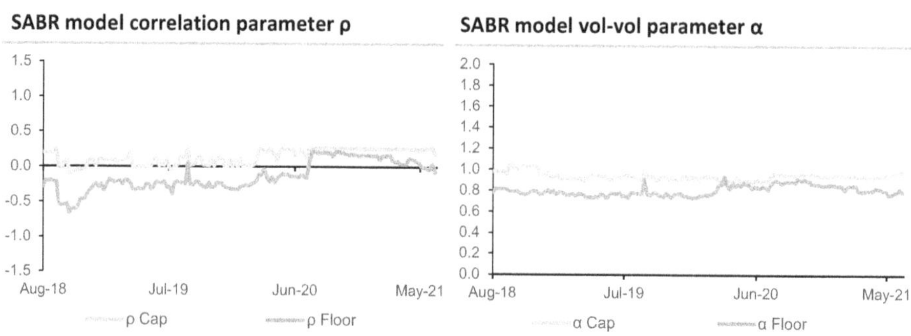

Figure 7.5: SABR model parameters ρ and α.
Source: Commerzbank Research.

While we would not expect the cap and floor parameters to be identical, it is reassuring as to the quality of the fit that they are similar, as we see in Figures 7.5 and 7.6. What is notable is that ρ, the correlation between volatility and rate level, is close to zero, and α, the volatility of volatility, is close to 1. Because if $\rho = 0$ and $\alpha = 1$, the SABR distribution collapses to a normal!

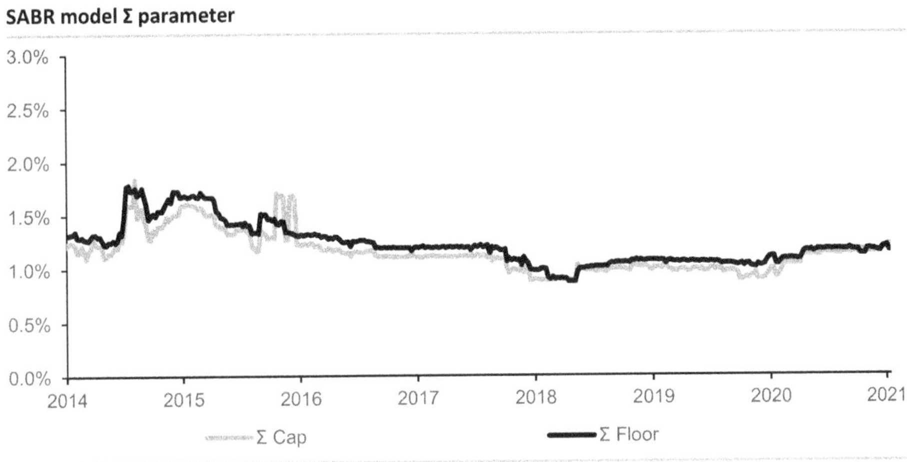

Figure 7.6: SABR model Σ parameter.
Source: Commerzbank Research.

"We Have Normality. I Repeat, We Have Normality. Anything you Still Can't Cope with is Therefore your Own Problem" (Adams 1979)

We have shown that the flexible SABR approach yields results for the EUR HICPx implied inflation pdf that suggests it is close to a (well-behaved) normal distribution. Additionally, the moments of the distribution beyond those needed for the normal are poorly fitted for the case of the USA CPI implied inflation pdf.

Having realized this, we can do some further investigations, for both cases.

Usefully, in addition to the distribution moments, the Minneapolis Fed dataset additionally contains the 10 percent, 50 percent and 90 percent probability levels. We know, of course that the 50 percent probability level is the same as the median of the distribution, so to decide whether skewness is important in this distribution, we can compare the mean and the median. Distributions where these two moments are the same are overwhelmingly likely to have minimal skewness.

To assess the likelihood of significant kurtosis, we compare the 10 percent and 90 percent probability levels with those obtained from a normal distribution with the identical mean and standard deviation from the same day in the data set. The results are shown in Figure 7.7.

The two graphs making up Figure 7.7 add up to a convincing case that there is no information in the Minneapolis Fed data set beyond mean and standard deviation, and that the distributions are normally distributed for all intents and purposes. Although it would be extremely useful to be able to compute skewness and kurtosis for the distributions, the sparse input data means that there is no real possibility of obtaining meaningful values for those moments.

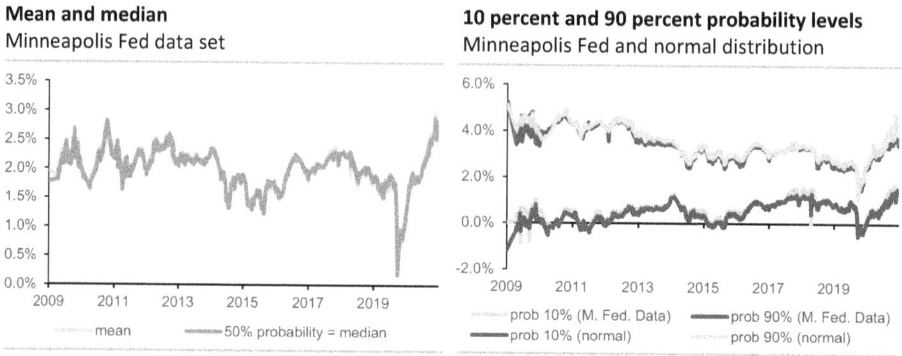

Figure 7.7: Minneapolis Fed results.
Source: Minneapolis Fed, Commerzbank Research.

Turning to the EUR HICPx distributions, fitted with the more flexible SABR model, the time series of its parameters α, β and ρ are already consistent with normality. In Figure 7.8, we plot the mean of the distribution through time, together with the SABR 10 percent and 90 percent probabilities, and those obtained from a normal distribution with identical mean and standard deviation equal to the SABR σ.

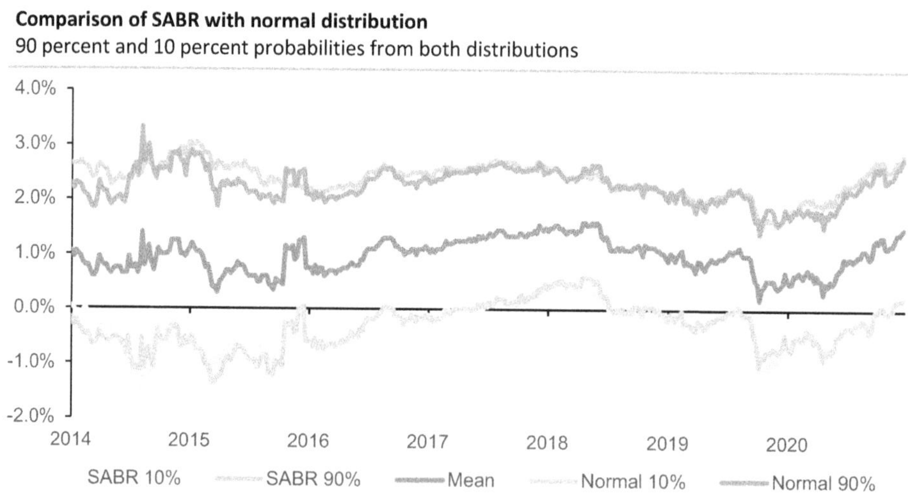

Figure 7.8: SABR vs normal distribution.
Source: Commerzbank Research.

Clearly, the distribution is as close to normal as makes no difference. What we are seeing is that, although the SABR model is perfectly capable of producing output distributions with skew or fat tails, the input data is consistent with a normal distribution, and indeed its sparse nature means that it is highly unlikely that meaningful values of higher moments could be extracted.

Put differently, the quoted caps/floor prices themselves seem to be based on a normal distribution, and irrespective of the sophistication of the model/function applied it seems primarily an inter/extrapolation exercise from a limited set to active points on the grid.

Is Inflation Normally Distributed?

Is it a problem that inflation options appear to assume that inflation is following a normal distribution? This would of course not be the case if actual inflation does follow a normal distribution.

To establish empirically whether this is the case, one needs a very long time series with annual inflation rates.

The euro area HICPx data only goes back to 1995, and it is not possible to make any firm statements on the underlying distribution, although eyeballing a simple histogram suggests a skewed distribution, as we see in the left chart of Figure 7.9.

More interesting in that regard is an analysis of inflation for the US, where CPI data goes back to 1914 (Figure 7.9, right chart), or the UK, where the BoE provides data back to 1209 (Figure 7.10).

It is worth a note on the eight centuries of BoE data – this has been painstakingly compiled from many sources and represents the best estimate of inflation over the years. While one might say that data from before the Wars of the Roses is not necessarily relevant to today, the fact that we now enter uncharted territory with the current inflation environment argues that an examination of data over a huge range of different scenarios has value.

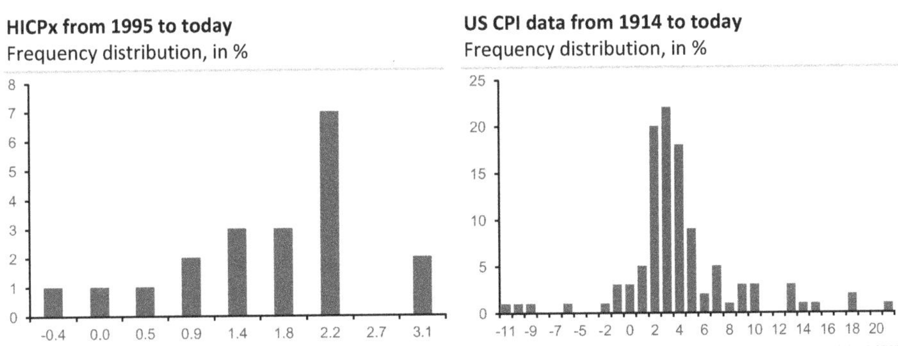

Figure 7.9: Long term HICPs and US CPI data.
Source: Bloomberg, Commerzbank Research.

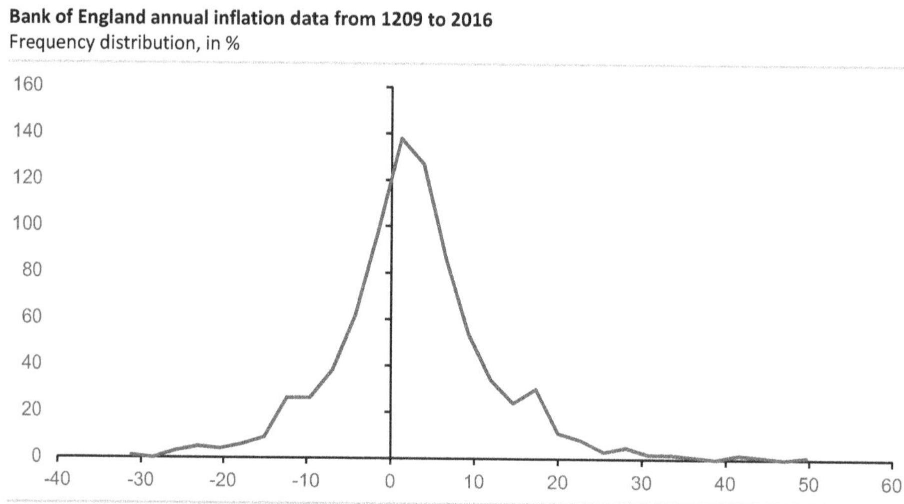

Figure 7.10: Long term GBP data.
Source: Bank of England data set, Commerzbank Research.

Analyzing this data in Table 7.2, we find that for the two longer term series at least, there is enough data to find higher moments of the distributions with standard errors low enough to give us some confidence in the results.

Table 7.2: Analyzing long-run inflation series.

	Mean	Standard Deviation	Skewness	SD(Skewness)	Kurtosis	SD(Kurtosis)
HICPx, N=19	1.50%	0.92%	−0.533	0.274	−0.059	1.029
US CPI, N=106	3.20%	4.83%	0.742	0.055	3.406	0.216
BoE, N=807	1.31%	9.40%	0.503	0.007	2.600	0.030

Source: Commerzbank Research.

It is extremely interesting that for both the US CPI and the BoE, their values for skew (slightly positive) and kurtosis (somewhat fat tailed) are similar to each other, and adds weight to the idea that a "correct" inflation distribution ought to deviate from the normal distribution to an extent. This is backed up by a working paper from the ECB (ECB 2007), which finds that US SPF inflation forecasts show strong asymmetry with a positive skew.

Thus, our finding that euro HICPx option valuations assume that inflation is following a normal distribution weakens the reliability of the implied probability distributions. Considering that in EUR the deflation floor is probably the most actively traded point given its importance for HICPx linkers, some caution is required for higher strikes/the right tail.

Commerzbank SABR Output Compared with Other Data

It is interesting to compare the SABR output with other data – below are the mean, 10 percent and 90 percent probability levels for HICPx five years ahead from the ECB Survey of Professional Forecasters (ECB 2021b), which comes out each quarter, with a quarterly smoothing of the same SABR quantities.

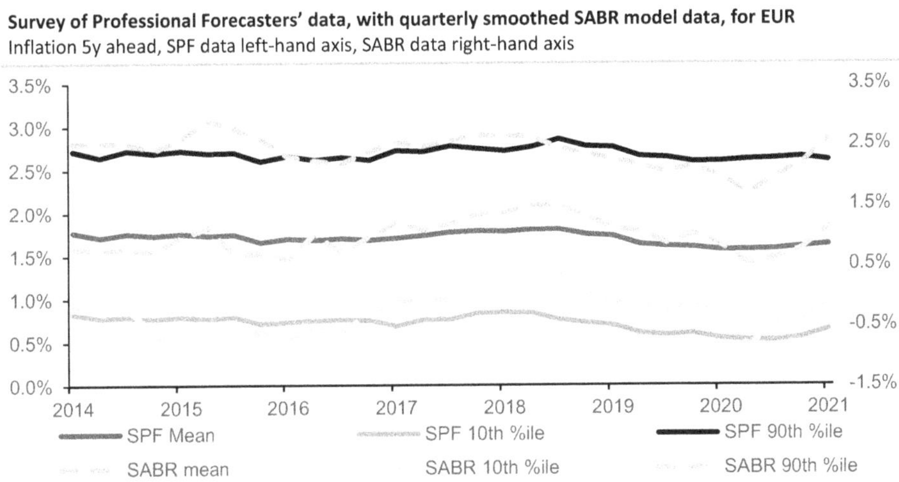

Figure 7.11: SPF and SABR data.
Source: ECB, Commerzbank Research.

We see in Figure 7.11 that there is an approximate agreement as to overall level, though the SABR results have a slightly wider range of anticipated outcomes. These differences are not surprising as options comprise risk-neutral probabilities and therefore do not reflect the true distribution given the existence of risk premia. They also refer to HICP ex tobacco, which is typically 7bp lower than headline HICP.

Finally, we can do a similar exercise with the US data. This time we take the quarterly CPI forecasts for 5y ahead, from the US Survey of Professional Forecasters, compiled by the Philadelphia Fed. They give the mean and the 25th and 75th percentile probabilities, and we perform a similar comparison to that in the previous graph, comparing their figures with a quarterly smoothing of the option-derived Minneapolis Fed data. The SPF data is on the left axis in Figure 7.12, with the option-derived data on the right axis.

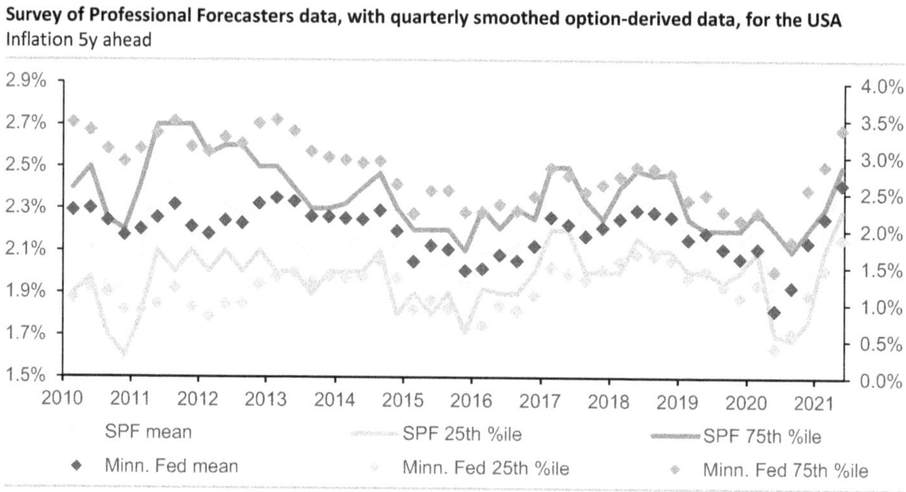

Figure 7.12: US SPF and inflation option data.
Source: Philadelphia Fed, Minneapolis Fed, Commerzbank Research.

As before, there is broad agreement as to the mean of the distributions, and more activity and dispersion for the option-derived data. It is also notable that for both the survey- and the market-based USD measures, the ranges are much lower compared to EUR, that is, the degree of inflation uncertainty seems notably lower in the US than in the euro area.

Liquidity Issues: Normal In – Normal Out!

It is apparent that the sparse availability of input option data means that there is little chance of calculating valid estimates of higher moments than mean and standard deviation. However, even the data that is available has significant fluctuations in liquidity and can often be very stale. The deflation floor is actively traded, but quotes on strikes away from this level are often mechanically generated levels from brokers, rather than actual trades. This being the case, it begs the question, how do these quotes get calculated? Hazarding a guess, it is unlikely that the brokers do more than use a simple model to generate them – and they probably use a normal distribution. This is absolutely consistent with all our findings above – if the SABR model, for example, is given data that is clearly skewed or fat tailed, it will represent this in its final output. But, if all it has to work on was originally generated from a normal distribution . . . well, normal in, normal out!

Conclusion

With the global inflation regime on the cusp of possible change from lowflation to a more dynamic and much higher zone, the markets are minutely focused on the probability of large moves. However, we have shown that the inflation option market is not liquid or granular enough to extract reliable tail or skew probability parameters beyond the normal distribution. So, it would be wise to treat estimates of large moves derived in this way with a good deal of caution.

Bibliography

Abrahams, M., Adrian, T., Crump, R.K., Moench, E. and Yu, R. (2016) "Decomposing real and nominal yield curves." *Journal of Monetary Economics* 84: 182–200.

Adams, Douglas (1979) *The Hitch-Hiker's Guide to the Galaxy*, Pan Books, London.

Adrian, T. and Wu, H.Z. (2009) "The term structure of inflation expectations." Staff Report, No. 362, Federal Reserve Bank of New York, New York.

Andreasen, M.M., Christensen, J.H.E. and Riddell, S. (2017) "The TIPS liquidity premium." Working Paper, Federal Reserve Bank of San Francisco 2017–11.

Auckenthaler, J., Kupfer, A. and Sendlhofer, R. (2015) "The impact of liquidity on inflation-linked bonds: A hypothetical indexed bonds approach." *North American Journal of Economics and Finance* 32: 139–154.

Bank of England (BoE) (2012) "Bank of England Quarterly Bulletin 2012 Q3." BOE, https://www.bankofengland.co.uk/quarterly-bulletin/2012/q3/option-implied-probability-distributions-for-future-inflation

Breeden, Douglas T. and Litzenberger, Robert H. (1978) "Prices of state-contingent claims implicit in option prices." *The Journal of Business* 51(4): 621–651.

Burban, Valentin, De Backer, Bruno, Schupp, Fabian and Vladu, Andreea Liliana (2021) "Decomposing market-based measures of inflation compensation into inflation expectations and risk premia." ECB Economic Bulletin 8.

Campbell, John Y., Sunderam, Adi and Viceira, Luis M. (2017) "Inflation bets or deflation hedges? The changing risks of nominal bonds." *Critical Finance Review* 6: 263–301.

Chen, R., Liu, B. and Cheng, X. (2010) "Pricing the term structure of inflation risk premia: Theory and evidence from TIPS." *Journal of Empirical Finance* 17(4): 702–721.

Chernov, M. and Mueller, P. (2012) "The term structure of inflation expectations." *Journal of Financial Economics* 106(2): 367–394.

Christensen, J.H.E. and Gillan, J.M. (2012) "Could the U.S. Treasury benefit from issuing more TIPS?" Federal Reserve Bank of San Francisco Working Paper Series 2011–16.

Christensen, J.H.E., Lopez, J.A. and Rudebusch, G.D. (2010) "Inflation expectations and risk premiums in an arbitrage-free model of nominal and real bond yields." *Journal of Money, Credit and Banking* 42: 143–178.

D'Amico, S., Kim, D.H. and Wei, M. (2018) "Tips from TIPS: The informational content of Treasury inflation protected security prices." *Journal of Financial and Quantitative Analysis* 53: 395–436.

European Central Bank (ECB) (2005) "ECB Monthly Bulletin." January, https://www.ecb.europa.eu/pub/pdf/mobu/mb200501en.pdf

European Central Bank (ECB) (2007) ECB Working Paper, no. 825, October.

European Central Bank (ECB) (2017) Gonzalo Camba-Mendez and Thomas Werner, "The inflation risk premium in the post-Lehman period." ECB Working Paper, 2033, March, https://www.ecb.europa.eu/pub/pdf/scpwps/ecbwp2033.en.pdf

European Central Bank (ECB) (2021a) "ECB blog regarding inflation dynamics in the pandemic," https://www.ecb.europa.eu/press/blog/date/2021/html/ecb.blog210401~6407b23d87.en.html

European Central Bank (ECB) (2021b) "ECB Survey of Professional Forecasters 2021," https://www.ecb.europa.eu/stats/ecb_surveys/survey_of_professional_forecasters/html/all_data.en.html

Fleckenstein, Matthias, Longstaff, Francis A. and Lustig, Hanno (2013) "Deflation risk." National Bureau of Economic Research, Working Paper, 19238, https://www.nber.org/system/files/working_papers/w19238/w19238.pdf

https://doi.org/10.1515/9783110787429-008

Grischenko, O.V. and Huang, J.-Z. (2013) "The inflation risk premium: Evidence from the TIPS market." *Journal of Fixed Income* 22(4): 5–30.

Hagan, P.S., Kumar, D., Lesniewski, A. and Woodward, D.E. (2002) "Managing smile risk." *Wilmott Magazine* 1: 84–108.

Hordahl, P. and Tristani, O. (2014) "Inflation risk premia in the euro area and the United States." *International Journal of Central Banking* 10(3): 1–47.

James, Jessica (1994) "Nuclear structure effects in atomic parity non-conservation," D.Phil thesis, the University of Oxford.

Kajuth, F. and Watzka, S. (2011) "Inflation expectations from index-linked bonds: Correcting for liquidity and inflation risk premia." *Quarterly Review of Economics and Finance* 51(3): 225–235.

Kim, Don, Walsh, Cait and Wei, Min (2019) "Tips from TIPS: Update and discussions." FEDS Notes May 21.

Kitsul, Yuriy and Wright, Jonathan H. (2013) "The economics of options-implied inflation probability density functions." *Journal of Financial Economics* 110(3): 696–711.

List of Abbreviations

€QE, €QE2	the first and second round of Quantitative Easing by the European Central Bank (ECB)
ASW	asset-swap
AuM	Assets Under Management
BE	Belgium
CMS	Constant Maturity Swap
CPI	Consumer Price Index
CSPP	corporate Sector Purchase Program, a bond buying exercise by the ECB
CTD	cheapest to deliver
DMO	debt management office
DV01	Dollar Value of one basis point
ECB	European Central Bank
EE	Estonia
EMU	Economic and Monetary Union
EONIA	Euro OverNight Index Average
EX	Spain
FI	Finland
FR	France
FRIx	French CPI ex tobacco (Indice des prix à la consummation)
GE	Germany
GR	Greece
HICPx	Harmonised Index of Consumer Prices ex. Tobacco
ILB	index-linked Bond
ILB	Inflation-Linked Bond
ILS	Inflation-linked swaps
IR	in the context of inflation products IR stands for Index Ratio. This is confusing as in the context of investment outcomes it is used for Information Ratio. In this book the first definition is the one used.
IR	Ireland
IRP	inflation risk premium
IRR	internal rate of return
ISDA	International Swaps and Derivatives Association
IT	Italy
LI	Lithuania
LV	Latvia
LX	Luxembourg
NL	Netherlands
NPV	net present value
OLS	Ordinary Least Squares
OOH	Owner Occupied Housing
OTM	out of the money
PCE	personal consumption expenditures
Pdf	probability distribution function
PEPP	Pandemic Emergency Purchase Program
PPI	producer price index
PT	Portugal
PVBP	present value per basis point

https://doi.org/10.1515/9783110787429-009

SABR	stochastic alpha, beta, rho
SAF	seasonal adjustment factors
SAP	seasonally adjusted price
SK	Slovakia
SMA	Survey of Monetary Analysts
SP	France
SPF	Survey of Professional Forecasters
SV	Slovenia
TIPS	US Treasury Inflation Protected Security
VAT	value-added tax
ZC	Zero-Coupon

List of Figures

https://doi.org/10.1515/9783110787429-010

List of Tables

https://doi.org/10.1515/9783110787429-011

About the Authors

Jessica James is a senior quantitative researcher at Commerzbank in London, and previously was head of the Quantitative Solutions Group. She joined Commerzbank from Citigroup where she held a number of FX roles, latterly as global head of the Quantitative Investor Solutions Group. Prior to this, she was the head of the Risk Advisory and Currency Overlay Team for Bank One. Before her career in finance, James lectured in physics at Trinity College, Oxford. She holds a BSc in physics from Manchester University and a D. Phil. in atomic and nuclear physics from Oxford University.

Her significant publications include the *Handbook of Exchange Rates* (Wiley), *Interest Rate Modelling* (Wiley), and 'Currency Management Overlay and Alpha Trading' (Risk Books). Her book *FX Option Performance* came out in 2015. She has been closely associated with the development of currency as an asset class, being one of the first to create overlay and currency alpha products.

Jessica is a visiting professor both at University College London and at Cass Business School. She is a managing editor for *Quantitative Finance*. Apart from her financial appointments, she is a fellow of the Institute of Physics and has been a member of their governing body and of their Industry and Business Board.

Christoph Rieger is heading the Rates & Credit Research at Commerzbank. Together with his research teams, he covers the full range of fixed income products, from money markets, government bonds and SSAs to covered bonds, financials and corporates, developing big-picture themes alongside commercial trading and funding strategies.

Prior to this role, Christoph was Head of Rates Strategy at Commerzbank and he worked as senior interest rate strategist at Dresdner Kleinwort with a specific focus on money markets and interest rate derivatives. Before joining Dresdner Kleinwort in 2004, Christoph held various positions in fixed income research, starting in 1998 at Commerzbank as a government bond analyst before moving to London in 2001, where his main focus was on interest rate strategies using derivatives. His academic background is rooted in economics, in which he holds two degrees: an MA from Temple University (Fulbright Scholarship in Philadelphia, PA) and a diploma from the University of Cologne (Germany). Christoph is a member of the ECB Bond Market Contact Group.

Michael Leister is responsible for interest rate strategy at Commerzbank. His research team of four analysts covers the full range of liquid and structured rates products for the major currencies, in cash as well as in derivatives space.

Michael joined Commerzbank London in 2012 with a focus on € rates and global inflation markets, after working as Interest Rate Strategist for WestLB in Düsseldorf and London with a focus on government bonds.

He holds a masters degree in economics from the University of Mannheim and has been awarded the CFA charter in 2012. Beyond financial markets he is a frequent participant in city and mountain marathons (PB 2:47).

https://doi.org/10.1515/9783110787429-012

About the Series Editor

Moorad Choudhry is an independent non-executive director at Recognise Bank Limited, a non-executive director at the Loughborough Building Society and a non-executive director at the Wandle Housing Association. He is Honorary Professor at University of Kent Business School. He was latterly Treasurer, Corporate Banking Division at The Royal Bank of Scotland.

Moorad is a Fellow of the Chartered Institute for Securities & Investment, a Fellow of the London Institute of Banking and Finance, a Fellow of the Global Association of Risk Professionals, a Fellow of the Institute of Directors and a Freeman of The Worshipful Company of International Bankers. He is author of *The Principles of Banking* (John Wiley & Sons 2012, 2022).

Moorad was educated at Claremont Fan Court school, University of Westminster and University of Reading. He obtained his MBA from Henley Business School and his PhD from Birkbeck, University of London. He was born in Bangladesh and lives in Surrey, England.

https://doi.org/10.1515/9783110787429-013

Index

https://doi.org/10.1515/9783110787429-014

The Moorad Choudhry Global Banking Series

Principles of Green Banking: Managing Environmental Risk and Sustainability
by Suborna Barua

Reverse Stress Testing in Banking: A Comprehensive Guide
by Michael Eichhorn, Tiziano Bellini, and Daniel Mayenberger (eds.)

Bank Asset Liability Management Best Practice: Yesterday, Today and Tomorrow by Polina Bardaeva

Random Walks in Fixed Income and Foreign Exchange: Unexpected Discoveries in Issuance, Investment and Hedging of Yield Curve Instruments
by Jessica James, Michael Leister, and Christoph Rieger

Banking Associations: Their Role and Impact in a Time of Market Change,
by Sladjana Sredojevic and Milan Brkovic

Inflation-Linked Bonds and Derivatives: Investing, Hedging and Valuation Principles for Practitioners
by Jessica James, Michael Leister, and Christoph Rieger

www.degruyter.com

www.ingramcontent.com/pod-product-compliance
Lightning Source LLC
Chambersburg PA
CBHW080939240926
51849CB00004BA/498
9783110787375